T0129730

A Short History of Heaven

Heaven in the Early History
of Western Religions and Today

JOANN GREIG

BALBOA.
PRESS

A DIVISION OF HAY HOUSE

Scripture quotations are from the New Revised Standard Version Bible, copyright © 1989 the Division of Christian Education of the National Council of the Churches of Christ in the United States of America. Used by permission. All rights reserved.

Balboa Press books may be ordered through booksellers or by contacting:

Balboa Press
A Division of Hay House
1663 Liberty Drive
Bloomington, IN 47403
www.balboapress.com
1 (877) 407-4847

Because of the dynamic nature of the Internet, any web addresses or links contained in this book may have changed since publication and may no longer be valid. The views expressed in this work are solely those of the author and do not necessarily reflect the views of the publisher, and the publisher hereby disclaims any responsibility for them.

The author of this book does not dispense medical advice or prescribe the use of any technique as a form of treatment for physical, emotional, or medical problems without the advice of a physician, either directly or indirectly. The intent of the author is only to offer information of a general nature to help you in your quest for emotional and spiritual well-being. In the event you use any of the information in this book for yourself, which is your constitutional right, the author and the publisher assume no responsibility for your actions.

Any people depicted in stock imagery provided by Getty Images are models, and such images are being used for illustrative purposes only. Certain stock imagery © Getty Images.

Print information available on the last page.

ISBN: 978-1-9822-0078-7 (sc)
ISBN: 978-1-9822-0079-4 (hc)
ISBN: 978-1-9822-0080-0 (e)

Library of Congress Control Number: 2018903389

Balboa Press rev. date: 03/27/2018

Contents

Climbing the tree of lights

We are so agile, no matter our age,
as we make our way up to the stars.
The ancient tree with roots deep in the ground
lifts us higher and higher.
It's a Christmas tree with a star on top or
it's Jacob's ladder with all the angels
going up and down.
Their messages abound.
Dreams of light playing through mist
by magical star bright, our cheeks are kissed.
We're no longer earth bound,
We're meant for flight,
Our souls fly upward into the night.
Soaring higher, we're covered with feathers,
and under His wings we shelter from bad weather.
And we too will flourish like fragrant cedars
planted in His house forever.
We will bear fruit for years to come,
fresh and green under the sun.

Joann Greig
Pristina, 2017

Introduction

This book has been a long time coming. I pitched the idea of researching the history of heaven in Western religions to my academic supervisor on October 28, 2010. A full seven years later to the day, I signed up with Hay House to publish this book, based on my research into the history of heaven. I had already graduated with my master of arts degree in cultural astrology and astronomy at the University of Wales Trinity Saint David. This had been a full seven-year cycle.

Initially, I thought the topic of the history of heaven was a fascinating research project. But I didn't realize that over the ensuing seven years, both my sister, Julie, and my father, Boyd, would have passed away, as well as several friends. I learned that what happens to people after their life on this earth is finished is not just an interesting research topic but of vital personal concern when it comes to those we are close to, as well as when confronting our own limited life span on this earth.

My interest in religion and the afterlife had begun well before that. In May 1995, I was in Egypt for a conference, and afterward was able to visit the Egyptian Museum for the first time. It was an awe-inspiring experience to see the golden treasure from the tomb of King Tutankhamun. I had grown up as a child looking at my parents' lavish travel and history books with colorful photographs of Tutankhamun's sarcophagus and other items from his tomb. I personally encountered that golden sarcophagus in the Egyptian Museum, and it exceeded the most extravagant photos I had seen of it. It was truly breathtakingly beautiful, otherworldly, and created through craftsmanship I would have never imagined to have existed in ancient times. The focus of ancient Egyptians in preparing for the death of their royal family, and maintaining them in the afterlife, had given rise to a culture, the remnants of which continue to fascinate and intrigue us today: the Great Pyramids of Giza, the elaborate tombs, the art and craftsmanship, and the embalming rituals. I entered one of the smaller pyramids at Giza, beneath the stars painted on a still-vivid blue sky deep under the earth; above the ground a statue of a pharaoh with eerily empty eyes stood among the dry rocks and shifting sands, intended as a vessel from which the spirit of the pharaoh could look out upon the world.

Most of us are familiar with stories from the book of Exodus in the Old Testament, or the Hebrew Bible. The Bible gives an account of how the baby Moses, who was discovered by the daughter of the pharaoh abandoned among the reeds of the river Nile, was brought up as Egyptian royalty. As an adult, he led his people, the Hebrews, out of their servitude in Egypt, eventually after many trials in the desert in finding the Promised Land. When I was in Jordan for a work meeting, I took the opportunity to visit some local sites of interest close to Amman, including the archaeological park at Jerash and Mt. Nebo. Mt. Nebo was said to have been the last resting place of Moses, from where he was said to have viewed the Promised Land after many years of wandering with his people, but he regrettably was unable to enter it himself. Standing on top of that mountain in the small church, I felt a personal sense of connection with the Bible story in that landscape.

While I stood there, I felt the first stirring of a Christian faith, which was to develop further later. I had an intuition that Jesus Christ himself had once stood on that same spot. It was a very different experience from hearing about his life at Sunday school classes in suburban New Zealand, many years earlier when I was growing up. Those accounts seemed far removed from what suddenly felt like a compelling reality. Standing on Mt. Nebo, I sensed the powerful divine revelation from some two thousand years earlier, rooted in the Hebrew tradition going back thousands of years before that. Many years later, I visited a special exhibition of Dead Sea Scrolls from Qumran in New York, organized by the government of Israel in collaboration with the United States. It included a large piece of the wall from Jerusalem. The exhibition gave me a sense of immediacy in my connection to the wisdom of those ancient scrolls, far from the place where they originated.

About ten years later, I was fascinated to study, again with the Sophia Centre at the University of Wales Trinity Saint David, a system of belief that had once rivaled early Christianity in the Roman empire—the Mysteries of Mithras. By the second century AD, the Mysteries of Mithras had become popular among the Roman legions and spread through the Roman empire until it declined after Constantine's conversion to Christianity in the fourth century. For a course on archaeoastronomy, which is archaeology with a focus on astronomy, I chose to study the orientation of the underground sanctuaries of the mysteries of Mithras, known as Mithraea. I was living in Austria at the time, and my first stop was the Carnuntum archaeological park, which was a short drive outside Vienna. This had been the regional capital of a Roman Province and included the sites of two Mithraea. While I could study notes and diagrams from when they were first excavated, and also visit museums containing artifacts that had been discovered there, I was unable to enter the Mithraea themselves, which were closed. However, I could get a sense of the way people lived in ancient Roman times, through walking the excavated and reconstructed villas, bath houses, streets, and even a large amphitheater where gladiators had competed. I learned that the great Roman philosopher and ruler Marcus Aurelius had lived there and had written his famous philosophical meditations. Regular historical reenactments are held at Carnuntum, and it was thrilling to see people dressed as Roman legionnaires and soldiers marching under the legions banners. The mysteries of Mithras were once very popular among Roman soldiers and administrators.

However, to find Mithraea that were still intact and open to the public at their original locations, I had to travel further afield to

Slovenia. I was able to visit two such sites, which had been excavated, covered, and left more or less in their original condition. It was fascinating to enter the sacred space where the mysteries of Mithras had been observed in Ptuj and to see the temple firsthand, with its parallel seating benches for initiates, statues, and the altar, including the famous image of the deity Mithras slaying a bull. Ptuj is a town in northeastern Slovenia and is the oldest recorded city in that country. It had developed from a Roman military fort. I learned that the Roman soldiers who belonged to the cult of Mithras had been passionate about exploring a possible afterlife in symbolic terms and had imagined and reenacted their souls' journey to heaven and back during their rituals. I wondered if those mysteries had somehow been a precursor to Christianity, and perhaps what the Roman soldiers experienced in those subterranean temples prepared them to later spread that faith under the Holy Roman Empire.

Fast forward through several centuries of history, and during a visit to the United Kingdom, I took the opportunity to visit the cathedral city of Wells, in Somerset, Southern England. There I experienced the Wells Cathedral Choir singing for Evensong. The choir has been at the heart of worship at the cathedral since the ninth century. The music had a timeless beauty, and I felt transported into the heavenly realms. As I was to discover in the course of my study of the history of heaven, for centuries, listening to sacred music was believed to be a way for people to come closer to the angels and even to the very gates of heaven itself.

I learned that through history in the Western world, people longed to know what happens in the afterlife and to find out about the destiny of their loved ones and themselves in the hereafter. As Job is quoted as asking: If mortals die, will they live again (Job 14:14)?

I wanted to know how these early beliefs were reflected in Christianity, if at all. Could I discover common threads or patterns between these ancient beliefs and more modern religions in the West? This book is an attempt to answer that question. Activities are included after most chapters to assist the reader to discover a little more about their own understanding of heaven, keeping in mind what we know of the beliefs of the ancient peoples. I have focused intentionally on the history of the religions that may be seen as precursors to Christianity. There are, of course, different traditions in the world concerning heaven and the afterlife that are found among faiths other than the ones examined here. They might have some remarkable parallels to those explored in this book, but limitations of time and space do not allow me to do them credit here.

Chapter 1

Concepts of Heaven

Ideas about heaven have appeared throughout history. Jeffrey Burton Russell, American historian and religious studies scholar, in *A History of Heaven,* observes that heaven, a concept that has shaped much of Christian thought and attitudes, has often been neglected by modern historians.[1] Christianity has played a central role in the West and instructs believers to direct their lives in this world with a view to achieving eternal life in the next.[2] It is of the greatest importance that many people see their apparently imperfect physical lives as just a stage in their progress toward a world that is perfect but invisible, yet it is often neglected as a subject.

Some believe that the most important aspects of the concept of heaven are the beatific vision and the mystical union. Heaven, Russell says, is the state of being in which all are united in love with one another and with God. Furthermore, Northern Irish theologian Alister Edgar McGrath notes at least one common theme that unites all these different visions and purposes.

> The Christian concept of heaven is iconic, rather than intellectual—something that makes its appeal to the imagination, rather than the intellect, which calls out to be visualized rather than merely understood.[3]

On the other hand, Professor of Hebrew Bible and Early Judaism J. Edward Wright[4] maintains that to understand the heavenly realm as imagined by early Jews and Christians, we must begin with an appreciation of the images of the heavenly realm found in the texts of these two religious communities: the Hebrew Bible. And to understand the broader social context, we must also examine the beliefs of ancient Israel's neighbors.

So what do we need to do to enter heaven? Is faith in the divine needed to reach heaven, or is personal moral responsibility needed, or is special knowledge of magical techniques needed to attain heavenly realms? Might elements of older religions be found in Christianity? What is the relationship between heaven and earth? What are the most important concepts about heaven?

This book takes the reader on a journey through ideas of heaven from early antiquity, through the time periods covered by the Bible, and up to the Nicene Creed in CE 381. We look at areas of similarities and differences among concepts of the cosmos, the soul, the soul's journey into heaven, and the relevance of morality. The term *Western* is used to include the Jewish and Christian traditions along with the religions in ancient Egypt, Persia, Mesopotamia, Greece, and Rome. Shamanism is used as a framework for indigenous traditions involving the soul's flight to the heavenly realms, notably in Siberian traditions.

The Hebrew and Christian Bibles provide us with insights into Jews' and Christians' understandings of heaven. Noncanonical texts also provide insights into early attitudes, including Gnostic traditions. Literature concerning concepts of the heavenly realm, from the neighboring cultures of Egypt, Mesopotamia, Persia, Greece, and Rome, are also examined.

We define religion as the worship of, or ritual interaction with, divine beings of anthropomorphized natural forces.[5]

Ideas about heaven are important today too. In September 2012, when I was living in New York, at an Episcopal church the pastor started an informal think tank to discuss heaven, with reference to Neale's book about her near-death experience: *To Heaven and Back.*[6] Participants raised many questions about heaven, especially regarding personal survival after death and being reunited with loved ones. Yet it was not quite clear how this could take place. Some people felt that heaven and hell were experienced by people while they were alive on earth.

I discussed Jewish concepts of heaven with an orthodox rabbi living in Brooklyn in June 2012, over a shared meal with his family and friends. The rabbi explained that after death, every Jewish soul would go to paradise. However, first a soul may need to be refined in hell or a concept similar to purgatory (Gehenna, the burning ground) as a temporary process. After death, angels show people a replay of their lives so they can judge themselves. Then the angels assign the deceased to their intermediate destinations, which may be Gehenna or heaven, which is a stage between death and the Messianic era. When the Messiah comes, the ultimate stage of human destiny is the resurrection of the dead, when souls will return to their immortal bodies for eternity.

Ultimately, it is about bringing heaven to earth, rather than people going permanently to a spiritual heaven. The rabbi explained that resurrection takes place not only for Jewish people but also for any good person who follows the seven laws of Noah and takes every opportunity to help others. The Noahide Laws are seven moral imperatives said to have been given by God as a binding code for all humanity. These are the prohibition of idolatry, murder, theft, sexual immorality, blasphemy, and eating flesh taken from a living animal; also included is the establishment of courts of law.

In popular culture, there have been several movies on the theme of people returning to earth from heaven on unfinished business. A classic of the genre is Warren Beatty's 1978 fantasy-comedy *Heaven Can Wait*, based on a 1941 movie called *Here Comes Mr. Jordan*. An American football player dies prematurely in an accident and aided by his guardian angel, returns to earth in the body of a recently deceased millionaire. Hilarity ensues, and through a series of events, the hero lives on in another body and resolves the pending issues he had on earth.

There has also been a steady stream of books on life after death and so-called near-death experiences. An example of this is Raymond Moody's *Life after Life*, a collection of stories told by people who have purportedly come back from the dead, having been medically pronounced dead and then resuscitated. While some may consider that this is the result of the high mortality rate during World War II and people's anxieties about the future after 1939, as we will see, human beings have been preoccupied with the afterlife for considerably longer than that. Clearly, heaven is an important topic for today.

Activities

What do you think will happen in the hereafter?

Is the idea of heaven important to you?

Chapter 2

Shamanism and the Upper World

Perhaps some of the earliest views of heaven, including soul flight, can be found in shamanism. The Siberian term *saman* (shaman) has been known in the West for at least three hundred years. Mircea Eliade, Romanian historian of religion, in his book *Shamanism: Archaic Techniques of Ecstasy* (2004), introduced an early understanding this phenomenon by defining shamanism as "techniques of ecstasy." During trance, the shaman's spirit is believed to leave his body and ascend to the sky, descend to the underworld, or travel in the middle earthly realm. This shamanic flight implies a sacred three-layered cosmology: the upper world, the earth, and the lower world. The shaman's spirit was thought to travel through these planes inhabited by spirit-beings. For example, Tamang shamans maintain that they magically fly through heavens and underworlds, where they encounter gods. Shamans often utilize a variation of an axis mundi, a central axis linking the realms, often represented by a cosmic tree, sacred mountain, or ladder. According to Eliade,

> The pole (= axis mundi), the stripped tree trunk whose top emerges through the upper opening of the yurt (and which symbolizes the cosmic tree) is conceived as a ladder leading to heaven.

5

Common shamanic initiatory rites enumerated by Eliade include a period of seclusion, symbolic descent to the underworld, and hypnotic sleep induced by narcotic drinks or awaiting a vision of the tutelary animal following intoxication by a psychoactive substance. Shamanic power is supposedly derived directly from gods, ancestors, or spirits, as well as master shamans.

The Tungus people saw a central pillar, based on the North Star, as a stable cosmic polar axis connecting heaven with the earth and the underworld. The shamanic world view includes an upper sky realm, the earthly middle world, and the underworld, all containing spirits that can interact with people. It was thought that the Tungus shamans made contacts with spirits as hunters and gatherers of supernatural power. Similarly, the final initiation of the Tamang shamans represents the soul's journey to the highest heaven to behold the supreme deity enthroned at the top of a golden staircase. Eliade explains how different places could enable the ascent of the shaman, including the cosmic mountain, which a future shaman might climb in a dream during his or her initiatory illness and visit on later journeys. It was a frequent theme that a future shaman would fall seriously ill and have a series of powerful dreams or visions that equipped him or her for later service to the community as a seer and healer. The World Tree also frequently appears in folklore of the peoples of central and north Asia, among others. The tree connects the three cosmic regions, with its branches touching the sky and its roots going into the underworld.

C. Michael Smith, clinical psychologist and anthropologist, in his book *Jung and Shamanism in Dialogue: Retrieving the Soul, Retrieving the Sacred,* comments:

> The magic tree is what the shamans mount in their journeys to the upper world, or descend via roots to the underworld. It is the axis mundi, at once a symbol for the center of the world, a symbol for the center of the psyche, the center point of orientation.[7]

We see a modern fictional depiction of a sacred tree as the center of the world, and *axis mundi*, in the movie *Avatar* (2009). An army base of the alien world, Pandora, is called "Hell's Gate," perhaps suggesting a connection with the underworld and that the hero will learn how to rise up through the worlds like a shaman. The "Tree of Souls" is the most sacred place on Pandora, which provides access to ancient ancestral wisdom and power. An alien female (Na'vi) Neytiri leads the hero from earth, Jake Sully, to learn about the power of the sacred tree in that world and to battle threats against it.

Some people have seen elements of shamanism in early forms of Christianity. For example, Paul's blinding "road to Damascus" spiritual experience and his reported ascent to the heavens could be consistent with shamanic vision and flight.[8] His outer sight is removed by the spirit, and he gains his inner sight through the experience. Paul's conversion experience is described in the Acts of the Apostles and his letters in the New Testament. Before his conversion, Saul, as he was then called, was a zealot and a Pharisee who persecuted the followers of Jesus. In Acts 9, he tells his story in the third person, relating that as he neared Damascus on his journey, suddenly a light from heaven flashed around him. He fell to the ground and heard a voice ask him, "Saul, Saul, why do you persecute me?" The voice revealed that the speaker was Jesus, whose followers Saul had indeed been persecuting. When Saul got up, he found that he had lost his physical sight and was blind. Upon reaching Damascus, he did not eat or drink anything for several days until his sight returned (see Acts 9:3–9). This dramatic experience led to the conversion of Saul to a follower of Christ and his transformation into the apostle Paul.

Some have understood Paul's religious life by comparing his experiences with shamanism, and his effectiveness in promoting the growth of Christianity being due to demonstrations of spiritual power, comparable to those of a shaman.

Shamanism, as conceived of in the West, has concepts of heaven parallel to those that may be seen in religions, such as an individual's ascent into the heavenly realms with help from spirit beings or angels. Furthermore, the qualifications for ascent may be a combination of special techniques and privileged interactions with spirit-beings or angels. This offers a framework for a person's journey to the heavens, as envisaged in the Judeo-Christian tradition and other cultures.

Activities

Think of a tree that has been important in your life.

When you are near the tree, or think about it, do you have a feeling of being close to the earth, as well as close to heaven?

Chapter 3

Ancient Egypt and Early Antiquity

Understanding the broader social context in which early Jewish and Christian ideas of heaven developed begins by examining the beliefs of ancient Israel's neighbors.[9] Here we consider the concepts of heaven prevalent in the groups that influenced early Jewish people (i.e., ancient Egypt, Mesopotamia, and Persia).

Ancient Egypt participated in ancient Near East culture and influenced its neighbors, including the people of Israel. The *Pyramid Texts* from the Old Kingdom (2686–2160 BCE) consist of prayers and rituals that helped the pharaoh in his after-death journey into the celestial realm.

> They made a ladder for (the Pharaoh), that he might
> ascend to heaven on it. The double doors of heaven
> are open for (him).[10]

From the Middle Kingdom (2040–1633 BCE), the *Coffin Texts*[11] are inscribed inside coffins to guide the deceased through the dangers of the afterlife. The *Pyramid Texts* and the *Coffin Texts* were revised and expanded during the New Kingdom (1558–1085 BCE) in a funerary collection known as the *Book of the Coming Forth by Day* or the *Book of the Dead*.[12] Nicholas Campion, British historian of astrology and cultural astronomy and director of the Sophia Centre for the Study of Cosmology in Culture at the University of Wales Trinity Saint David, observes that the soul, the *Ba,* might travel either to the sun's rising, to Orion, or the circumpolar stars to achieve immortality.[13] After a ritual has been properly performed, the individual is seen as "risen and made whole," and he enters a new glorified life, conceived of in physical terms, such as being able to eat and drink.[14]

According to ancient Egyptians, there are three main regions in the cosmos: the earth—the land of the living; the sky—a watery expanse stretched above the earth like a canopy; and the Duat—the otherworld or the underworld. The realm above the earth could be depicted in four basic forms: a bird, a cow, a woman, and a flat plane. A depiction of the goddess Nut from 323–30 BCE represents the goddess as she bends over the earth, with dual heavens comprising the sphere of the moon and the upper Nut as the sphere of the sun. Another depiction of the heavenly realm is a pastoral paradise known as the Field of Reeds. The Duat is a complex otherworldly region, including Osiris and the kingdom of the dead. According to the ancient Egyptians from this period, beyond the sky, earth, and Duat lies the limitless expanse of primal waters.

The Field of Reeds is described in three statements in the *Book of the Dead* (110, 109, 149) as a landscape of waterways leading through fields where abundant crops grow, in a place where gods and the blessed dead live in peace. It contains islands, mounds, fields, pathways, caves, creatures, and fantastic elements, such as lakes of fire and trees of turquoise. Mounds of sand and gravel rising above the flood plain signified the primeval mound that first emerged from the waters of chaos.

The path of the sun, moon, and planets, which the Egyptians called the "Winding Waterway," divided the sky into northern and southern parts. The northern sky contained the Field of Rest (or Offerings) and the southern sky the Field of Reeds. In the *Pyramid Texts*, the deceased are purified in the Field of Reeds before ascending to the sky, but in the *Coffin Texts* the Field of Reeds becomes a destination for the deceased, as in the *Book of the Dead*. In the *Book of the Dead*, it is not clear whether the Field of Reeds is located in the sky or under the earth, but according to Utterance 149, it seems to be in the east at the point where Ra was believed to end his nightly journey. It resembles the Nile flood plain at harvest time and is similar to the best locations of the earth. Utterance 110 describes ploughing, reaping and eating, drinking, and having sex in the field.[15] The deceased are reunited with their parents, and then they sail to meet the gods. Any work that is needed is believed to done by the small figures placed in the tomb to serve the needs of the deceased. The tomb provides access between the world of the living and the dead for the mummy in the burial chamber. This marks the body's transition from an "inanimate corpse to a functional complex of physical and spiritual components."[16] The ability to "come forth by day" (i.e., for a spirit to leave the tomb) is crucial in these funerary traditions.

The Egyptian *Book of the Dead* describes multiple gates through which the deceased pass to reach Osiris. The procedure for passing through seven gates is by correctly saying the names of fierce guardians. The deceased then review their lives before Osiris, including the weighing of the heart. Thoth, the God of learning and magic, asks ritual questions.

"Why have you come?"

"To be anointed."

"What is your condition?"

"I am free of every sin."

"To whom shall I announce you?"

"To him whose ceiling is fire, whose walls are living uraeii (sacred serpents), whose house floor is the flood."

"Who is that?"

"Osiris."

(Taylor, 206–7)

The deceased should answer correctly and declare themselves to be innocent of a list of offenses to avoid punishment, which suggests that the tests may have originated in priestly initiations (e.g., "I have not stolen the gods' offerings"). The deceased, led by psychopomp Anubis, the canine-headed Egyptian god associated with death and the afterlife, would then be judged in the "Weighing of the Heart" (Utterance 125) against a feather of the Goddess Ma'at, embodying truth and justice. If the scales balance in favor of the virtuous heart of the deceased, the gods assign them a good afterlife. Utterance 30B of the *Book of the Dead* guards against the heart of the deceased admitting to sins, so ritual knowledge enables the destiny of the deceased to be safeguarded. However, if all does not go well, the deceased is given over to a wrathful entity called "the Devourer" for punishment.

According to Mark Smith, professor of Egyptology at the University of Oxford, in the "Democratization of the Afterlife," *Encyclopedia of Egyptology,* the ancient Egyptian concept of the human being comprised a physical self and a social self, as the individual could only function as a member of a properly structured society. Death severed the links between parts of the body as well as between the individual and his social group. The God Osiris provides a model by which this rupture could be reversed, as Osiris had undergone resurrection and restoration. The Egyptian *Book of the Dead* states "Heaven hath thy soul (*ba*), earth hath thy body,"[17] which could be interpreted as meaning that the soul has the freedom to enter heaven. Just as Osiris overcame the injustice of his murder in Egyptian mythology, so did ancient Egyptians hope to achieve immortality through the embalming process. Furthermore, a favorable assessment of the deceased's character during the weighing of the heart ritual would ensure his or her integration into the world of gods and blessed spirits in the afterlife (see Mark Smith, in the "Osiris and the Deceased," *Encyclopedia of Egyptology*). These rituals were believed to make the deceased a follower of Osiris and gain admission to his presence in the underworld.

According to Campion, the ancient Egyptian funereal texts

could be interpreted as ecstatic rites that were to be conducted while still alive, in which the king while living, shaman-like, traveled spiritually to the sun and stars to maintain his kingdom's link between heaven and earth.[18] Furthermore, the Egyptian notion of cyclic time may have made it possible to bring an experience of the future into the present, so that the realities of death and the afterlife could be experienced or imagined in this life. The Egyptian concept of nonlinear cyclic divine time without a sharp temporal distinction between life and death could allow for a process culminating in which the individual is believed to assume the likeness of the sun god.[19] The ancient Egyptian cosmos was a moral one with divine judgment of the condition of the heart as a key to the afterlife. However, mystical technology and magical mastery was an essential ingredient for reaching the desired destination, not merely moral rectitude.

Activities

Imagine that your heart is being weighed against the feather of truth. Is it lighter or heavier?

What do you need to do to live closer to your heart's truth?

Chapter 4

Ancient Mesopotamian Traditions

Mesopotamian beliefs from the late third millennium to the middle of the first millennium BCE provide another context for biblical beliefs. The creation myth the *Enuma Elish* records Mesopotamian beliefs about the basic structure of the cosmos in three parts: the heavenly realms (of the high gods), earth (realm of humans), and the netherworld (of the deceased and mortuary gods). Heaven is subdivided into three levels comprised of different-colored stone, two terrestrial worlds, plus the underworld.[20]

Sumerians built their temples on the summits of artificial hills or ziggurats, where a person is believed to be appearing before the God in heaven. There, the priests performed divination by observing the sky to obtain information from the gods. "Sky and earth both produce portents though appearing separately, they are not separate (because) sky and earth are related."[21]

The Mesopotamians saw the grave as the final destiny of humankind. Punishment for evil deeds was believed to come during our life on earth, not in the afterlife, and there was no concept of humans uniting with the gods in heaven after death. "When gods created humanity, they appointed death for humanity and kept life in their own hands."[22]

The earthly paradise of Dilmun is normally reserved for gods, with the exception of the legendary figure of Ziusudra who, like Noah, survived the great Flood and was transferred there. Etana, the first king after the Flood, asked an eagle to carry him to the heavenly realms to obtain the "plant of birth" that would provide a dynastic heir. The poem emphasizes the vast chasm separating heaven and earth. Humans have no place in the divine, heavenly realm, and even the great antediluvian king Etana was forced to declare, "I cannot go up into heaven!"[23] As Gilgamesh said, "Who can go up to heaven, my friend? Only the gods dwell with the Shamash forever. Mankind can number his days. Whatever he may achieve, it is only wind." This is paralleled by Ecclesiastes 4:16: "Surely this also is vanity and a chasing after wind."

High gods are considered to be living as part of a divine assembly in heaven, where they decide the fate of gods and men. Ultimate power and authority was believed to reside with the chief God, similar to an earthly king. The *Kirta Epic* states that El is the chief God in the Ugaritic pantheon, presiding over the other gods in the Council of El. However, in the *Baal Cycle*, Baal replaces El as Chief God. Among Iron Age (1200–586 BCE) Israelites, Yahweh is the chief God of the divine council (see 1 Kings 22:19–23; Job 1–2).

Activities
Like the Babylonian priests who climbed to a high place to better study the sky for omens, look up at the sky. See the shapes that clouds make. Can you see images, like a racing horse or a rearing dragon? Is there a message for you today?

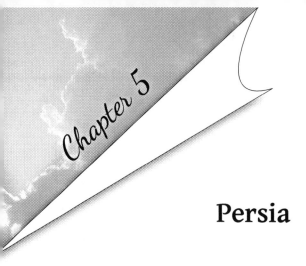

Chapter 5

Persia

The book of Daniel of the Bible records that the Persians occupied Babylon in 539 BCE and that the Jewish prophets were influenced by the religion of their new rulers. The religion of ancient Persia, current-day Iran, Zoroastrianism, holds that the material world is a theater for struggle between good (Ahura-Mazda, the good God) and evil (Ahriman, the evil god). Before the teachings of Zoroaster, it was believed that after death, the spirit of the deceased lingered on earth for three days before departing to a subterranean kingdom to live a shadowy existence, depending on their living descendants to satisfy their needs through ritual offerings. Later, some members of higher social groups might ascend to "cross the separator" bridge to heaven. Unworthy souls attempting the passage would fall off the bridge into the kingdom of the dead. Furthermore, the concept of bodily resurrection was important in Zoroastrianism:

> With the hope of attaining Paradise there developed a belief in the resurrection of the body ... it came to be held that within the first year after death the bones of the physical body would be raised up, clothed in immortal flesh, (and) be reunited with the soul in heaven.

> —Mary Boyce. *Zoroastrians: Their Religious Beliefs and Practices*

Eventually, people of all classes hoped to attain Paradise based on each soul's ethical achievements. Mithra (deity of truth and judgment) was believed to preside over the tribunal of gods, holding the scales of justice that weigh the soul's thoughts and deeds. If good prevails, the soul is judged worthy of Paradise; however, if the scales sink to the negative side, a monster takes the deceased to hell.[24] Those few souls whose bad and good qualities are in balance go to a place where they lead a gray existence lacking both joy and sorrow.[25]

The story of the soul's journey from death to the afterlife is contained in the Middle Persian or Pahlavi text *Dastan-i Menok-i Krat*.[26] The bodily resurrection is followed by the Last Judgment, to divide the righteous from the wicked. The soul then unites with the "future body."[27] All the metal on earth will melt, and humankind must pass through a river that will destroy the wicked. Then Ahura Mazda and the gods will make the mystical *soma*, believed to confer immortality on the resurrected bodies of the blessed in a garden Paradise.[28] Soma is an intoxicating juice from a plant of disputed identity that was used in ancient India and Persia as an offering to the gods and as a drink of immortality by worshipers in ritual.

A heavenly journey was recorded in myth as being undertaken by the high priest Kartir (third century CE), who reported, in a now fragmentary form, the existence of heaven and hell. Psychotropic drugs were taken in a ritualistic setting to help the adept travel to the next world, and prayers were used to protect the journeyers from harm.[29] The *Book of Arda Viraf*[30] contained a similar account. Arda Viraf is chosen by a drawing of lots to travel to heaven and learn ways of resolving the crisis caused by the arrival of Alexander the Great. He is given a special drug to enable him to visit heaven and hell, the respective abodes of the deceased, both righteous and sinful. Possibly the soma, believed to be prepared by the gods and that conferred immortality, was based on the practice of taking psychoactive substances to facilitate visionary experiences. According to Viraf, the visionary journey to heaven to seek wisdom from the gods is the same as that undertaken upon death. In heaven, Viraf finds a "star track," a "moon track," and a "sun track," where he sees the souls of different kinds of righteous people, for example:

> I put forth the first footstep to the star track … the place where good thoughts are received with hospitality. And I saw those souls of the pious whose radiance … was glittering as the stars; and their throne and seat were under the radiance, and splendid and full of glory. And I asked Srosh the pious, and Adar the angel, thus: 'Which place is this? And which people are these?' (They) said thus: 'This place is the star track; and those are the souls who, in the world, offered no prayers … exercised no … rulership or chieftainship. Through other good works they have become pious.[31]

Still higher in the heavenly realm, he encounters the creator god Ohrzmad, orders of angels, and other groups of the blessed. At the conclusion, Ohrzmad instructs Viraf to exhort the world to piety and performance of good works.

Zoroastrian doctrines include the judgment of individuals based on how they lived their lives, post-mortem destinations of heaven and hell, the resurrection of the body, the last judgment for the populace, and immortality for people's reunited soul and body. The achievement of a blissful afterlife for the individual depends on the sum of his or her thoughts, words, and deeds, without the possibility of any intervention from a divine being to alter this. On the day of judgment, each person has to bear responsibility for the fate of his or her own soul.

Activities
On a clear night, it is a good idea to go to a place where there is not too much light pollution from city lights. Many resources can

be found to identify the constellations and the movements of the planets. Can you see the Milky Way, which can appear like a track of stars? It is awe inspiring to think that the ancients also looked up and encountered the heavens directly.

Chapter 6

Common Themes Regarding Heaven and the Afterlife

Some common themes emerge in the periods examined so far: gods live in the sky and affect what happens on earth. There is a separation of sacred (in the temple or heaven) and profane (mundane earthly space and activity). Furthermore, a tripartite concept of the universe was shared: the underworld, the earth, and an upper heavenly realm, having more than one part. Access to the gods in heaven is possible at sacred temple sites, which are often elevated, either naturally or as a temple in the form of a pyramid.

Images of heaven include a fertile plain, a garden, a royal court, and a place among the stars, sometimes having multiple levels. These levels contain a series of guarded gateways or portals through which it was necessary to pass to progress. Entrance to heaven could be gained by the correct conduct, rituals, or offerings. The complex funerary traditions of ancient Egypt may have been part of a ritual framework, through which initiates could experience the anticipated post-mortem state while still alive.

The use of psychoactive plants for trance induction has been widespread in cultures practicing shamanism and has been linked to the Indo-Aryan soma of Eurasia.[32] Their use in inducing a trance-state to undertake heavenly journeys is notable in the Zoroastrian tradition, and perhaps there is a connection with the gods' soma of immortality, which was expected to be given to the blessed after the final judgment and resurrection.

Activities

Enjoying a cup of hot chocolate using organic cocoa, a cup of coffee using freshly ground aromatic coffee beans, or perhaps freshly brewed green tea, while sitting in a garden or in the park, can give us a sense of being in an earthly paradise.

Chapter 7

Classical Greece and Rome

In this chapter, we examine the early concepts of heaven and the afterlife as expressed in the epic poetry of Homer and Hesiod, along with the concepts of judgement of the deceased in classical Greece and Rome based on our conduct during life and the afterlife. The writings of the Greek philosophers Plato, Pythagoras, and Aristotle were influential in developing later ideas of heaven in the afterlife. The Ptolemaic model of the cosmos also appears. The Ptolemaic kingdom was founded in 305 BC by Ptolemy I Soter, who declared himself Pharaoh of Egypt and created a Hellenistic dynasty over the area stretching from southern Syria to Cyrene and south to Nubia. The mysteries of Mithras are an example of teachings concerning the heavenly journey of initiates during this period. We can see the results of the interaction of Greek, Babylonian, and Egyptian culture in the Hellenistic period and compare these ideas of heaven with earlier concepts, particularly from Egypt and Mesopotamia.

Greek thought in the Homeric Age (around 1200–700 BCE), as expressed in Homer's *Iliad* and *Odyssey* and Hesiod's *Theogony,* viewed living people as dwelling on the earth, while the dead resided in Hades, the underworld. The *Odyssey* contains Odysseus's encounter with the shades or ghosts of Hades, a place "where there is no joy."[33] It was imagined that people only went to heaven through an exceptional act by the Olympian gods and goddesses,[34] but even in Homeric times, it was believed that after death, extraordinary mortals could go to the beautiful meadows of the Elysian Fields or the Isles of the Blessed, which were located at the ends of the earth:

> But for yourself, Menelaus, fostered by Zeus ... it is not ordained that you should die ... but to the Elysian plain and the ends of the earth will the immortals convey you ... where life is easiest for men.[35]

Orphism refers to religious beliefs and practices originating in the Ancient Greek world associated with the mythical poet Orpheus, who descended into the underworld and returned. Orphics also revered other divine figures who also were believed to have descended into the underworld and returned (i.e., Persephone and Dionysus). Pythagoreans and Orphics believed that after death the immortal soul attempted to reunite with the universal soul in the heavenly realm from whence it came. For example, Aristophanes, a Greek dramatist (450–388 BCE) confirms that people were believed to be turned into stars after death:

> Servant: Is it true, what they tell us, that men are turned into stars after death?
> Trygaeus: Quite true.
> Servant: And who is the star over there now?
> Trygaeus: Ion of Chios. The one who once wrote a poem about the dawn; as soon as he got up there, everyone called him the Morning Star.
> Servant: And those stars like sparks that plough up the air as they dart across the sky?
> Trygaeus: They are the rich leaving the feast with a lantern and a light inside it.[36]

Furthermore, Pindar, Greek lyric poet (ca. 518–438 BCE),

describes the judgment awaiting reckless souls and the rewards of the righteous:

> That the reckless souls of those who have died on earth immediately pay the penalty ... But ... the good receive a life free from toil ... Those who have persevered ... follow Zeus' road to the end, to the tower of Cronus, where ocean breezes blow around the island of the blessed, and flowers of gold are blazing.[37]

While, according to the early Greeks, Mt. Olympus and the heavenly realm were for the gods alone, by the fourth century BCE, the heavenly realm was considered to be a post-mortem residence. For example, a memorial to the Athenians who died in the battle of Potidaia in 432 BCE depicts their souls as attaining immortality after death: "the ether has received their souls, while the earth has their bodies."

Plato, a Greek philosopher living from 428/427–348/347 BCE, in *Timaeus* and the *Republic,* explains the soul's origin in, and return to, the stars, describing the earth as a sphere around which the planets and fixed stars revolve.[38] During his travels, Plato may have encountered purifying rites that blended together Orphism with the Eleusinian mysteries, Dionysiac worship, and Pythagorean belief, and perhaps these became his source for the concepts in *Phaedo,* where virtue purifies and wisdom is a purifying rite. "From Orphic rites and Eleusinian mysteries Plato derived the belief that the initiated, the purified, would ascend to the gods, while the uninitiated, the impure, would wallow in the mud."[39]

In *Phaedrus,* the soul originates above and the highest God is beyond heaven:

> For those that are called immortal, when they reach
> the top, pass outside and … behold the things
> outside of the heaven … the mind, the pilot of the
> soul … beholds absolute justice, temperance, and
> knowledge … abides in the real eternal absolute …
> after which, passing down again within the heaven,
> it goes home.[40]

In *Timaeus*, Plato says that souls are made by a deity (a subsidiary god known as the demiurge) in numbers equal to the stars: "And when He had compounded the whole He divided it into souls equal in number to the stars, and each several soul He assigned to one star."[41] The soul that is able to overcome its passions may return to its native star. This idea that each person's soul is linked to his or her own special star is one of the Plato's most evocative ideas.

In what might today be called a near-death experience, in Plato's Myth of Er in the *Republic*, the hero dies and his soul visits the underworld, as well as the heavens, where he witnesses souls being rewarded or punished according to their behavior on earth, before returning to tell others about what he experienced. According to Plato, through a process similar to reincarnation, which he called *metempsychosis*, souls choose new lives and drink from the river of forgetfulness called the River Lethe. They then continue on from the stars, through the planetary spheres, to be born on earth, while the three Fates, or Moirae, create the circumstances in which each person must live, by spinning the web of necessity.

An evil life leaves scars on the soul that can be seen by three judges who view souls. These judges, who are called Rhadamanthus, Aecus, and Minos, are stationed in the afterlife meadow at a place where two paths diverge, one to the Isles of the Blessed and the other to the underworld, or Tartarus.[42] Each soul's destination, good or ill, is determined by the judges examining their scars and deciding whether they are blessed, curable, or incurable. Each soul is then assigned to the appropriate place in the afterlife. The curables may go to a kind of prison in Hades, where they witness the suffering of others, and thus educated, they eventually enter the Isles of the Blessed (527d–e). The negative conduct includes: false oaths, lying, boasting, ugliness, arrogant power, insolence, and incontinence; while the righteous on the other hand live piously, with truth, minds his or her own business, is good and noble and practices virtue.

Marcus Tullius Cicero, Roman writer, lawyer, and orator's *Dream of Scipio,* illustrates a similar Roman belief that people find rewards in the heavenly realm for living a noble life. "To all those who have saved, succoured, or exalted their fatherland, there is assigned a fixed place in heaven, where they will enjoy everlasting bliss, for it is from heaven that they who guide and preserve states have descended, thither to reascend."

The ancient Greek philosopher Aristotle (384–322 BCE), in his treatise "On the Heavens," proposes that each of the heavenly bodies encircles earth in its own sphere. The heavenly realm from the ether, or outer reaches of space, down to the moon was characterized by perfection and unchanging order, while the lower realms closer to earth became increasingly disorderly. While Aristotle's cosmology was essentially atheist in nature, he shared Plato's belief that people inhabit an ordered cosmos in which they are directly connected with the stars and planets.

The geocentric model with earth at the center of the universe is most readily identified with the Greco-Roman mathematician and astronomer Claudius Ptolemy of Alexandria (ca. 100–170 CE), even though it was not solely his innovation. In this system, eight planetary spheres are associated with the seven planets and the fixed stars, as contained in Ptolemy's *Almagest,* a compilation of astronomical speculations and calculations. In this geocentric model, a stationary earth is situated in the center of the universe, encircled by planetary spheres that have the character of the respective celestial body, planet, luminary, or star it was named after.

Activities

Plato believed that every person had a special connection to a star. Do you feel a special connection to any particular star?

Whether I'm in the northern hemisphere or the southern hemisphere, on a clear night, I always look to see if I can spot the star Sirius. A few years ago, I did a tour in Egypt into the desert for the purpose of stargazing at night. We went in desert vehicles to a particularly dark area surrounded by hills to keep out the ambient light of the towns nearby, so we could observe the night sky in all its glory. Our local tour guide, a young Egyptian man, pointed to the star Sirius, which was shining brightly in the dark sky. He said that he believed that his spirit would go to that star in his afterlife.

Chapter 8

Mysteries of Mithras

The mysteries of Mithras were an influential spiritual movement throughout the Roman Empire, featuring a ritual representation of the soul ascending through the planetary spheres toward the heavenly realm, which were enacted to help initiates rehearse the ascent they expected to take in the afterlife while they were still living. By the second century CE, the Mithraic mysteries had spread throughout the Roman Empire, although they declined with the rise of Christianity in the fourth century.

Few historical records are available about the mysteries of Mithras, whose central iconography shows Mithras as a young man killing a bull with a knife, known as a Tauroctony. However, we can understand something about them from the buildings and art of the period. The writings of Porphyry, a neoplatonic philosopher (234–c. 305 CE), also provide important insights from a contemporary perspective. In his commentary *De Antro,* Porphyry writes:

> The ancients ... properly consecrated a cave to the world ... mystically signifying the descent of the soul into the sublunary regions, and its regression from it, (and there) initiate the mystic ... (the constellation of) Cancer is the gate through which souls descend; but (the constellation of) Capricorn that through which they ascend ... the southern

gates are not the avenues of the gods, but of souls ascending to the gods.[43]

Roger Beck, professor emeritus in classics, presented the Mithraic cave, or Mithreum, the underground temple where worshipers met, as a model of the cosmos that had the function of guiding the initiates up to heaven and then down to earth again along the "route of souls."[44] Furthermore, the "Mithras Liturgy"[45] text from the "Great Magical Papyrus of Paris" (Numbered *PGM* IV.475-834), includes a prayer intended to enable an initiate to ascend to the heavenly realm:

> "I request immortality, O initiates of this power …
> which the great God Helios Mithras ordered to be
> revealed to me by his archangel, so that I alone may
> ascend into heaven as an inquirer and behold the
> universe."[46]

As part of a broader context, the interaction of Greek, Babylonian, and Egyptian culture in the Hellenistic period resulted in a technical approach to the influence of the heavens, including the *Corpus Hermeticum*, core documents in the Hermetic tradition. The Hermetic tradition is a set of philosophical and religious beliefs based mainly on writings attributed to the legendary sage, Hermes Trismegistus. According to the Hermetic texts, the soul returns to God via the planetary spheres.[47] As it passes each sphere, the soul discards the vices associated with that planet; for example, as it passes the sphere of Mercury, it abandons trickery, Venus voluptuousness, Mars recklessness, and so on. The planets are depicted as administrators or custodians determining the heavenward progress of human beings.

As discussed below, Franz Cumont, Belgian archaeologist and historian, observes:

> All these doctrines … taught that souls, descended
> from the light above, were raised to the region of the
> stars, where they dwelt forever with these radiant
> divinities. This eschatology of "Chaldean" origin
> gradually displaced all others under the Empire. The
> Elysian Fields … located in the depths of the earth,
> were transferred to the ether which leaves the stars,
> and the subterranean world became henceforth the
> gloomy abode of malevolent spirits.[48]

In other words, as time went on, people became more likely
to imagine the afterlife in the heavens above, rather than in the
underworld below.

Discussion

In the Homeric Age (1100–800 BCE), Greek beliefs paralleled those
of Mesopotamia, in that human beings and gods were believed to
dwell in separate realms and that the deceased were consigned to
the underworld, with few exceptions. However, over time, the belief
developed that morally virtuous individuals resided in the heavenly
ethers after death. In Egypt, the nonphysical elements of the person,
along with his or her embalmed body, were believed to live on,
whereas in Greece, only the psyche was believed to survive death.
The soul was thought to go through a purgation or cleansing before
returning to a physical body through a process of metempsychosis
or reincarnation, unless it right away achieved the highest reward
of passing to heaven or the soul deserved punishment in Tartarus;
whereas, in Egypt, there was only a happy afterlife or deserved
suffering.

The judging of souls in Plato's *Gorgias* shows that the moral
conduct of the deceased while alive determines their post-mortem
state, as in Persia and Egypt. The passing of a soul through the
planetary spheres to reach the fixed stars, in some ways, paralleled the
passing of the soul through the Egyptian Duat gateways, to attain

immortality through magical knowledge and personal integrity. Furthermore, Taylor suggests that the Field of Reeds could have been the origin of the Elysian Fields, as "Elysian" may have been derived from the Egyptian word for reeds. The belief that the blessed find their place among the stars parallels the Zoroastrian "star track" and other celestial realms, as well as the journey of Arda Viraf, which, in some ways, resembles the journey in the *Myth of Er*.

The complex interaction between different elements of each individual in ancient Egypt differs from the Greek notion of the soul that separates from the physical body at death and could be reborn on earth, which also has no parallel in Mesopotamian beliefs. While in Virgil, *Aeneid*, book VI, describes the Elysian Fields as being in Hades, Homer locates them at the end of the earth by the Oceanus River. Also, the location of the Field of Reeds is not clear. In addition, the Greek doctrine of metempsychosis, has no parallel in Mesopotamian beliefs. However, the notion that the soul and stars are inextricably linked underpins several concepts of human post-mortem destiny.

Judaism

Jewish beliefs about heaven through the biblical period to the end of the apocryphal period are reviewed here. Judaism developed in a cultural milieu with a keen interest in celestial events and their influence on earthly life. Its views of the cosmos further developed from the dynamic interaction between ancient Near Eastern and Hellenistic models of the cosmos. The traditions of Merkabah (meaning "chariot" in Hebrew, involving heavenly journeys in a mystical chariot) and Hekhalot (from the Hebrew word for palaces, involving heavenly journeys to mystical palaces) include accounts of heavenly journeys by remarkable Jewish sages, as well as elaborate descriptions of the heavenly realms and the magical expertise needed to undertake them. The prophet Enoch is an early model for the ascension of an individual to heaven and his or her transformation into an angelic being (angelification). We also consider possible parallels with Greek and Persian thought concerning heaven, the afterlife and dualism.

The first book of the Hebrew Bible, Genesis 1:1, states: "In the beginning God created the heavens and the earth," indicating the primacy of heaven and the duality of sky and earth in creation. This became part of a tripartite structure—heaven or sky above, earth in the middle, and the netherworld (*sheol*) below as is shown in the following commandment: "You shall not make for yourself an idol, whether in the form of anything that is in heaven above, or that is on the earth beneath, or that is in the water under the earth" (Exodus 20:4). The Hebrew word *samayim* can be translated as "heaven" or "sky." Its suffix "*-ayim*" signifies plurality, suggesting two or more heavens or the sky's vast expanse. The floor of heaven is composed of stone: "they saw the God of Israel. Under his feet, there was something like a pavement of sapphire stone, like the very heaven for clearness" (Exodus 24:9–10). As the source of rain and weather, on the day the Great Flood started "all the springs of the great deep burst forth, and the floodgates of the heavens were opened" (Gen. 7:11).

God is depicted as a mighty king, simultaneously dwelling in his Jerusalem temple and in his heavenly palace. (See for example, 1 Kings 8, 21:1; 2 Kings 20:18.) Furthermore, the celestial realm is populated with the "host of heaven" (Jeremiah 33:22), which is a vast assembly of celestial beings. The appellation "Yahweh of Hosts" identifies God as the commander-in-chief of a heavenly army. He also acts as a divine judge: "God has taken his place in the divine council; in the midst of the gods he passes judgment" (Psalm 82:1). Since God dwells in heaven, the term *heaven* becomes associated with the divine name.

Around the seventeenth or sixteenth centuries BCE, the family tomb became central to understanding the hereafter. The deceased King Solomon is described of having "slept with his ancestors" as described in 1 Kings 11:43, and Jacob gives instructions for his future burial with his own kin (see Genesis 49:29–31, 33). Sheol, as the land of the dead, is depicted as cavernous and all-consuming (e.g., Isaiah 5:14), where ghosts or shades live. However, between the tenth and eighth centuries BCE, scripture begins to indicate that God can save people from Sheol, as in Psalm 49:15. Sheol becomes viewed as an intermediate resting place for the righteous and a permanent abode for the wicked.

Before the first century BCE, heaven or paradise (*pardes* is Hebrew for "orchard") is considered the abode of Enoch and Elijah, who had never died but rather ascended to the heavenly realms, becoming models for later ascensions. Later, heaven emerges as the dwelling place of the righteous following the last judgment, which is separate from Sheol as the place for the wicked (Jubilees 7:29, 22:22, 24:31). The doctrine of the resurrection of the dead paves the way for the notion of heaven and hell in Psalms, such as Psalm 50:4, and in the book of Daniel it is written:

> Many of those who sleep in the dust of the earth shall awake, some to everlasting life, and some to shame and everlasting contempt. (Daniel 12:2)

Hekhalot and Merkabah Traditions

The texts of the Apocrypha and the Pseudepigrapha provide further insights into Jewish ideas on the hereafter. The Apocrypha and the Pseudepigrapha are Jewish writings from the Second Temple Period (thirteenth–third centuries BCE) that are included in the Septuagint and Vulgate but excluded from the Jewish and Protestant canons of the Old Testament. The apocryphal texts ("apocrypha" is Greek for "hidden away") are not present in the Hebrew Bible, but have been included in the Septuagint (the Greek translation of the Bible), with some being included in the Catholic Bible. Collections of Jewish speculations in the *Hekhalot* ("palace") and *Merkabah* ("chariot") literature describe God as being enthroned in a celestial palace[49] with the throne as an image of absolute authority, which may seem alive (see Daniel 7:9). They tell tales of the journeys of sages through heavenly palaces or use the image of God's chariot. This tradition includes three important elements: the qualities of the ideal mystic, his heavenly journey, and his transformation at its conclusion.[50]

This literature is "apocalyptic" as defined by John J. Collins, professor of old testament criticism and interpretation at Yale Divinity School:

> a genre of revelatory literature with a narrative framework, in which a revelation is mediated by an otherworldly being to a human recipient, describing

a transcendent reality which is both temporal, insofar as it envisages eschatological salvation, and spatial insofar as it involves another, supernatural world.[51]

During the Apocryphal period, heaven comes to be seen as the resting place for deceased righteous individuals. The righteous will "shine like the lights of heaven, and you shall be seen; and the windows of heaven will be opened for you ... you will make a great rejoicing like the angels of heaven" (1 Enoch 104:2, 4). In the first book of Enoch, Enoch undertakes a journey through heaven and hell, while the second book of Enoch describes Enoch's ascent through each of the seven heavens, where mysteries are revealed to him, including the third heaven as a post-mortem realm (2 Enoch 8:1–8). The *Book of the Secrets of Enoch* was written in a Judaeo-Hellenistic environment during the first century BCE. Second Enoch 9 sets out the qualifications for entry into paradise:

> This place, O Enoch, is prepared for the righteous, who endure all manner of offence ... who avert their eyes from iniquity, and make righteous judgment, and give bread to the hungering ... walk without fault before the face of the Lord, and serve him alone, and for them is prepared this place for eternal inheritance.[52]

Third Enoch introduces a third class of deceased souls who are of intermediate merit and have the possibility of post-mortem purification. It is also known as *Sefer Ha Hekhalot—The Book of the Heavenly Palaces* or *The Hebrew Book of Enoch* and is attributed to the Palestinian rabbi Ishmael around the early second century CE.

While traditional Judaism sees the relationship between God and humanity as divinely initiated and manifesting through the Torah, the Hekhalot and Merkabah traditions emphasize personal mystical encounters with God and the heavenly realms that are initiated by human beings.[53] Students are encouraged to record the accounts of the mystics to transmit esoteric teachings to the Merkabah group.[54]

After the destruction of the temple in 70 CE, some Jews within these mystical circles continued temple worship in a different way by mystically visiting a surrogate heavenly temple instead of physically doing so.[55] This experience was achieved through methodical meditation and mystical contemplation, as described for example in the manuals of Abulafia such as "The Book of Eternal Life" written in 1280 and "The Light of Intellect" written in 1285. To ascend safely, the rabbis had to perform purifying rituals and memorize passwords to obtain safe passage from angels. Candidates had to meet certain criteria for gaining admission: possession of moral qualities, facial and other physical qualities, such as hand shape, criteria, and knowledge of related topics. Rabbi Gershom Scholem, in his *Major Trends in Jewish Mysticism* (New York: Schocken Books, 1946 (1995)), views this as a variation to second- and third-century Gnosticism and Hermeticism, with the ascent of the soul past challenging angels to its divine hom, signifying redemption. This journey is preceded by ascetic practices for twelve to forty days, including recitation of prayers in a certain posture (head between knees). Increasingly complex magic seals and recitations to subdue hostile angels are needed for each new level, in a kind of passport procedure. The ascent becomes ever more dangerous, especially for the unworthy, as the angels challenge the traveler. The idea of the seven heavens through which the soul ascends after death or during a state of ecstasy is reflected in texts, such as the fourth book of Ezra or the Ascension of Isaiah. Hekhalot and Hellenistic mysticism have differing concepts of God: in the Hekhalot tradition, God is the Holy King of All, rather than an impersonal divinity.

The journeyers ascend to heaven in a chariot, up a ladder or on the wings of a divine being and experience a vision of God. An early model of the heavenly journey was provided by the prophet Ezekiel, who was reportedly lifted into a divine chariot and transported upwards by the wind (Ezek. 3:12–13), as well as Elijah, for whom: "there appeared a chariot of fire, and horses of fire ... and Elijah went up by a whirlwind into heaven" (2 Kings 2:11).

Rabbi Ishmael, a rabbinic sage of the first and second centuries, states that the journey, shaman-like, "is like having a ladder in one's house on which he ascends and descends and there is no creature who can prevent him" (*Hekhalot Rabbati; Synopse*, 199). Similarly, in Jacob's dream, he sees "a stairway set up on the earth with its top reaching the heavens" (Genesis 28:12). As recounted in Genesis, Jacob dreams that he sees the angels of God ascending and descending on the ladder, before experiencing the presence of the Lord God. In addition, 3 Enoch describes the existence of seven heavens, seven palaces, and angelic guards at each. In that account, Rabbi Ishmael, after ascending to the seventh palace, is rescued from the fierce gatekeepers by the angel Metatron (formerly Enoch), prince of the divine presence, who shows the rabbi the sights of heaven.

Divine Judgment and the Transformation of Enoch

The Jewish views of the unity of body and soul find expression in beliefs about bodily resurrection. Eschatological doctrines of divine judgment and the resurrection of the righteous form a baseline for their beliefs about the afterlife. "And when the whole of creation, visible and invisible, which the Lord has created, shall come to an end, then each person will go to the Lord's great judgment" (2 Enoch 65:6).

The apocryphal book 3 Enoch describes the post-mortem judgment of souls as taking place in a heavenly court of law, with the Holy One sitting in judgment on individuals after their deaths, rather than at the last judgment (*Hekhalot Rabbati; Synopse*, 199). It also suggests a method for reestablishing the harmonious relationship between the divine and humanity, which allows certain individuals to ascend to heaven into the presence of God. This book records the transformation of the human Enoch into Metatron, the angelic Prince of the Countenance. Enoch sheds his human form, becoming an enormous, winged, glowing figure and is granted a place in the celestial hierarchy, along with profound wisdom that enables him to guide other Merkaba seekers.

> *Third Book of Enoch*, states in the words of God: "I transformed his flesh into torches of fire, and all the bones of his body into fiery coals; and I made the appearance of his eyes as the lightning, and the light of his eyebrows as the imperishable light. I made his face bright as the splendour of the sun, and his eyes as the splendour of the Throne of Glory."[56]

The canonical basis for the belief that Enoch was transformed into an angel –since his death is not mentioned – is contained in Genesis: 'Enoch walked with God after the birth of Methuselah three hundred years … Enoch walked with God; then he was no more, because God took him'. (Genesis 5:22-24)

Elliot Wolfson, professor of Hebrew and Judaic studies, observes that Jewish sources, beginning with the Apocalyptic and Qumran texts, may provide model of mysticism based on the "angelification" of the human being who crosses the boundary of space and time and becomes part of the heavenly realm.[57] The mystical experience in this framework involves a two-step closing of the gap separating human and divine by the ascension into the heavens: (a) participation in the angelic liturgy in a standing posture, and (b) enthronement in the celestial realm, which represents the fullest expression of the mystical experience, an eschatological ideal of deification.[58]

According to Wolfson, the ultimate secret of the prophetic experience is the imaginative representation of the divine as an Anthropos, i.e., a primordial man or human being. Only one who transforms the physical body into something spiritual—a transformation that is presented as angelification—is capable of imagining the divine form in bodily images.[59] Wolfson explains rather than being merely a harmony between heavenly and earthly worshipers, mysticism involves the narrowing of the gap between human and divine: the ascension to heaven and transformation into an angelic being who occupies a throne alongside the throne of glory.[60] The mystical experience expressed in the Hekhalot thus involves a heavenly ascent culminating in the enthronement of the mystic that transforms him into an angelic being, a transformation that facilitates his vision of the glory and the powers of God.[61]

Wolfson states that to envision the glory, a term that signifies in Qumran fragments the heavenly world, "one must become glorious, aglow with the glimmer of the divine image, the angelic splendor in whose likeness Adam was created."[62] He refers to two principles, one traceable in the Greek philosophical tradition to Anaxagoras, "like sees like," and the other to the occult wisdom of hermetic alchemy, "like mirrors like," expressed in the Emerald Tablet attributed to Hermes Trismegistus, "What is below is like that which is above, and what is above is like that which is below, to accomplish the miracles of one thing."[63] A priest can behold the glorious light without only when he has become that light within, a transformation facilitated by faithful adherence to ascetic practices, especially sexual renunciation, intended to realize the ideal of ritual purity (Leviticus 15:17; see also Wolfson, *Seven Mysteries of Knowledge*, 193).

As Martha Himmelfarb, professor of religion at Princeton University, observes, a human being can become the equal of the angels standing at the center of a group of eight early Jewish and Christian apocalyptic texts in which ascent to heaven is the mode of revelation.[64] Enoch becomes an angel in a kind of priestly investiture, donning special garments and being anointed with oil by the archangel Michael, suggesting that the transformation of the visionary depends on an understanding of heaven as a temple, where angels are heavenly priests. Further implications of angelomorphism, the transformation of the human body into an angelic body, are discussed further in the following chapter in the context of the apostle Paul's writings and the Qumran liturgical texts.

Discussion

Parallels exist between parts of the Mesopotamian and Jewish traditions regarding the cosmic blueprint that divided the world into the celestial realm above, the earth, and the underworld. Both describe the firmament as being composed of precious stones. God rules the celestial hosts in heaven, apart from humans who dwell on earth, although the divine may be encountered through the sacred spaces of the temple. Jewish beliefs of the post-mortem underworld originally parallel those of ancient Babylon. Over time, however, blessed post-mortem conditions were considered available for more individuals meeting the required moral criteria.

The apocrypha and the pseudepigrapha texts describe the way qualified Hekhalot and Merkabah Jewish sages could travel in the celestial realms. Sometimes they show Hellenistic influences; for example, resembling elements of the *Myth of Er* and the charioteer in Plato's *Republic* and *Phaedrus*.[65] Parallels can also be observed with the Zoroastrian heavenly journeys, where sages, this time under the influence of psychotropic plants, make the journey to obtain wisdom.[66] Platonic influences may be observed in abstract notions of immortality of the spirit and joining with the stars in heaven, while other texts offer an elaborate view of the happenings in the celestial realm, using concrete imagery. The spirit of the deceased could come forth from the tomb with a properly embalmed mummy in Egypt or could be finally resurrected, in the case of the Persian or Jewish righteous.

The increasing duality of the Jewish Sheol or Gehenna (underworld or hell) contrasting with paradise/heaven as destinations of the deceased, coupled with the role of divine judgment in determining rewards or punishment, contains elements resembling aspects of Zoroastrianism. According to Alan F. Segal, scholar of ancient religions and former professor emeritus of religion, it is probable that

Zoroastrianism, Judaism, and Christianity had "cross-fertilized" one another in later periods, although he considered it likely that the kernel notion of resurrection was initially a Zoroastrian idea, as it appears in the earliest Persian literature. However, James Barr, Scottish biblical scholar, concludes that the Iranian Zoroastrian influence probably came to Judaism through the admixture of Oriental ideas in the Hellenistic world and was adopted as part of an anti-Hellenistic reaction from 170 BCE.[67] He found that convincing evidence of Iranian (or Persian) influence on earlier strata of the Old Testament was lacking. Barr suggests that the Jews might find stimulus in an element of Iranian religion, such as its dualism or its idea of resurrection, even though they might not have appreciated their meaning within Iranian religion itself

The transformation of the individual who approaches the higher heavenly realms into a being like an angel can be seen in the Jewish texts.

Activities

Many of our ideas about angels come from Jewish traditions and writings about them. One of the most beloved angels is St. Michael, otherwise known as Archangel Michael, and many churches are dedicated to him. Such churches often have statues or pictures showing St. Michael vanquishing a fierce dragon, illustrating his qualities as a protector. His name means "Who is like God?" in Hebrew, and St. Michael is mentioned three times in the book of Daniel in the Hebrew Bible. He also appears in the book of Revelation of the New Testament of the Christian Bible.

Check to see where there is a church dedicated to St. Michael near to where you live or in towns you might be visiting. It is well worth a visit to see the images of the archangel that may be found in such places.

I carry with me a coin from an inter-faith series of guardian angels from the Austrian Mint, depicting Archangel Michael, to remind me that divine protection is always available if we ask.

Christianity

This chapter examines the New Testament, which is the second of the two major parts of the Christian Bible. We consider cosmological elements originating in Judaism, as well as concepts concerning the eschaton. Particular attention is given to the writing of Paul the apostle, as being amenable to both orthodox and gnostic interpretations. His views concerning the transformation of the believer into a "citizen of heaven" are examined, including in the context of traditions based in the Dead Sea Scrolls from Qumran. The book of Revelation is examined as explaining what the believer can expect from the eschaton, the end of days, the conclusion of God's plan for humanity and the earth. We consider the role of layered interpretation of scripture and symbolism and ways this has been applied to the New Testament. This chapter culminates with consideration of the Nicene Creed as a widely accepted formulation of Christian beliefs concerning heaven and its relationship with earth.

Among its twenty-seven books, the New Testament contains recollections of the life and sayings of Jesus in the four gospels; a historical narrative of the first years of the Christian church in Acts of the Apostles; epistles or letters of instruction to groups of Christians; and an apocalyptic description of the eschaton, the book of Revelation. When Christians die, they go to heaven leaving behind their physical bodies, to be with Christ (2 Cor. 5:1–8; Luke 23:43); however, the New Testament does not depict this as their final destination. They do not receive immortal physical bodies until after the resurrection, which follows the pattern established by Jesus Christ as a prototype (2 Cor. 5:15; Thess. 4:13–17): he lived on earth as a mortal man, died, and was resurrected from the dead, ascended to heaven, and then returned to earth in a physical body. The central message of the gospel is that the *basileia,* or kingdom of heaven, is "at hand" or "near." Irenaeus, one of the most influential early church fathers, set out his vision of the final restoration of God's creation, emphasizing that it must be a physical resurrection, based on the promise that Christ will "drink the fruit of the vine with his disciples in some higher region above the heavens (*in supercaelesti loco*)."[68]

Abraham's bosom (or side) is featured in Jesus's parable of Lazarus and the rich man, where, upon death, the poor man was transported by angels to repose in Abraham's bosom, while the rich man was plunged into the torment of hell (Luke 16:19–31). Abraham's bosom was defined by the first Latin Christian writer, Tertullian, as follows:

> That region, Abraham's bosom, though not in heaven, yet not so deep as hell, will in the meanwhile afford refreshment to the souls of the righteous, until the consummation of all things makes complete the general resurrection with its fullness of reward.[69]

Paul the Apostle, Angelomorphism and the Apocalyptic Tradition

St. Paul (4 BCE– 62 CE), a prolific Christian writer and former Pharisee, was converted to Christianity through a religious experience, where he was blinded by a supernatural light—the so-called Road to Damascus experience. In 2 Corinthians 12, Paul describes his experience of ascending to the third heaven in the third person (i.e., as if it had happened to someone else), which is rooted in the Jewish apocalyptic traditions as discussed in the previous chapter:

> I know a person in Christ who fourteen years ago was caught up to the third heaven—whether in the body

or out of the body I do not know; God knows. And
I know that such a person—whether in the body or
out of the body I do not know; God knows—was
caught up into Paradise and heard things that are
not to be told, that no mortal is permitted to repeat.

Paul's ascension to the third heaven parallels the mystical
experiences of apocalyptic Jews. This ascension to heaven may also
be linked with the newly resurrected body, which is similar to, or the
same as, an angelic body, through a process that has been termed
angelification or angelomorphism.[70] A master narrative of salvation
is marked by a change in the structure of the human body into a
glorious body shared with Christ. For example, "But our citizenship is
in heaven, and it is from there that we are expecting a Savior, the Lord
Jesus Christ. He will transform the body of our humiliation that
it may be conformed to the body of his glory" (Philippians 3:20).
The Qumran Library and its liturgical worship texts provide us with
insights into pre-rabbinic Judaism and the cultural background of
early Christianity. The scrolls and scroll fragments recovered in the
Qumran area are a voluminous collection of Jewish documents,
dating from the third century BCE to 68 CE. They include the
earliest manuscripts of most of the Hebrew Bible books, apocryphal
or pseudoepigraphical (i.e., writings other than the canonical
books and the Apocrapha professing to be Biblical in character)
and sectarian scrolls associated with the Essene community. The
historical background of the Dead Sea Scrolls remains controversial,
with some of the documents resembling the precepts of the Essenes, a
Jewish group comprising a number of writers of the first century CE,
including Flavius Josephus and Philo of Alexandria.[71] Dated from
BCE or CE first century, they refer to divine angelic hierarchies and
God's throne chariot, similar to the Hekhalot tradition.

The *Songs of the Sabbath Sacrifice*, from Qumran (4QShirShab),
known as the *Angelic Liturgy,* describes the Sabbath worship of
the angelic priesthood in the heavenly temple. Each of the seven

firmaments described have their own sanctuary containing an inner chamber (holy of holies), with each being administered by its own high-priestly chief prince and secondary prince, also mentioning multiple chariots and thrones. The final inner chamber, the central throne room, is inhabited by God himself. The community believed that the righteous would be rewarded by "eternal blessings and everlasting joy in the life everlasting, and a crown of glory and a robe of honour, amid light perpetual" (1 QS 4:7–8), while sinners would be met with "eternal torment and endless disgrace … in the fire of the dark regions" (QS 5:12–13). Crispin Fletcher-Louis, biblical scholar, argues that the purpose of the language of mystical participation at Qumran is angelification. "The priesthood is a primary conceptual category for the formation of an angelomorphic identity."[72] The liturgy seems to map a seven-stage ascent to heaven to view God's throne and glory. Worship in the heavenly temple includes an example of angelomorphism in the blessing:

> May you be as an angel of the Presence in the Abode of Holiness to the Glory of the God of (Hosts).

> May you attend upon the service in the Temple of the kingdom and decree destiny in company with the Angels of the Presence, in common council (with the Holy Ones). (1QSb 4:24-28)

The angelomorphic status may have also implied the possibility of transport to what Corbin termed the imaginal realm.[73]

Crispin Fletcher-Louis, maintains that the purpose of entry into the sacred temple—of access to the heavenly world offered by the inner sanctuary—is *transformation*. Worship makes proximity to God possible along with conformity to his character and modes of action. The liturgical anthropology of the temple tradition is essentially a matter of *deification*.[74] Furthermore, a ritual connection between the celibacy of some Essenes and their angelomorphic identity is possible.[75] See, for example, Leviticus 15, which requires a man to ritually bathe after sexual discharge or contact to become ceremonially clean.

Furthermore, in connection with angelomorphism, the Old Testament describes Enoch's life, but not his death:

> Enoch walked with God after the birth of Methuselah three hundred years ... Enoch walked with God; then he was no more, because God took him. (Genesis 5:22–24)

The above represents the canonical basis for the belief that Enoch did not die but he was transformed into an angel in heaven (Metatron), as illustrated in Hekhalot literature. The idea of angelification also finds clear support in the Gospels of the New Testament:

> Jesus said to them, "Those who belong to this age marry and are given in marriage; but those who are considered worthy of a place in that age and in the resurrection from the dead neither marry nor are given in marriage. Indeed, they cannot die anymore, because they are like angels and are children of God, being children of the resurrection." (Luke 20:34–36)

Such themes have been further developed by the apostle Paul, by stating that the body of glory or pneumatic body becomes androgynous, regains its divine likeness, its angelic completeness. In addition, he describes the primal combination of male and female that is lost in the garden of Eden (Gen 2:10). As amplified by Paul:

> There is no longer Jew or Greek, there is no longer slave or free, there is no longer male and female; for

all of you are one in Christ Jesus. (Galatians 3:28;
also see Col. 3:11)

Fletcher-Louis also discusses angelomorphism in Luke's gospel
and the book of Acts. In Acts 6:15, the face of the martyr Stephen
is directly likened to that of an angel; and in Acts 12:13–15 it
is assumed that a person's guardian angel closely resembles that
person. He considers that those texts were constructed in conscious
interaction with Jewish traditions of human angelomorphism.[76]
According to Fletcher-Louis, the Lukan angelomorphic Christ
brings an angelic identity and status to his followers:

> The message in the Gospels and in the writings of
> Paul with respect to believers being transformed
> into either angelic beings, or beings analogous to
> angels, implies that a believer will undergo a radical
> transformation, which is a prerequisite to becoming
> a full citizen of heaven.

Paul, the traditionally assumed author of the book of Hebrews in
the New Testament, writes about another aspect of Jesus Christ's life,
which could also be connected to angelomorphism and speaks of its
possible connection with the priesthood at Qumran. He describes
Christ as "a priest forever according to the order of Melchizedek"
(Heb.5:6 with reference to Psalm 110:4). Melchizedek is a mysterious
figure in the book of Genesis (Gen. 14:18–20) who as "a priest of
God Most High," presents bread and wine to Abraham and blesses
him. Melchizedek does not belong to the traditional Levitical priestly
caste of the Israelites. Early Church Fathers understood this as
representing a pre-figuration of the priesthood of Christ and that of
the Catholic Church (see *The Catechism,* 1333). Paul describes Christ
as a high priest in the sanctuary and a true tabernacle, which was set
up by God (i.e., in heaven, Heb. 8:1–2). The theme has been further
amplified by Peter, who says: "But you are ... a royal priesthood ...

God's own people" (1 Peter 2:9). While in Revelation, John writes "you have made them to be a kingdom and priests serving our God" (Rev. 5:10). This is the notion that angelomorphism is linked to heaven as a temple, with angels serving as heavenly priests.

Angelomorphism can be understood in various ways, from literal to figurative, and has links to early liturgical practices, although the concept has been deemphasized in current Christian teachings. The nature of the angelification could imply that human beings: join the angels' worship in heaven and thereby become more angelic by association; change into an angelic class of being through a process of transformation with divine fire; begin to function as messengers (*aggelou*) of the divine due to their faith; or become identified with Jesus Christ in the resurrection, the radical and magical transition from an earthly level to a heavenly one, aided by ritual, ascetic, prayer, or other religious practices, which has been equated with angelification in both Jewish and Christian earliest traditions. Being "born from above" by mystical enthronement in sacred space is seen as another key to both the contemplation of the divine and the empowerment of the individual seer.

> Angelification can be understood in different ways: whether human beings join the angels' worship in heaven and become more angelic by association; change into an angelic class through transformation by divine fire; function as messengers (*aggelou*) of the divine due to their faith; or become identified with Jesus Christ in the resurrection. The radical transition from an earthly level to a heavenly one, aided by ritual, ascetic, prayer, or other religious practices, has been equated with angelification in both Jewish and Christian earliest traditions.

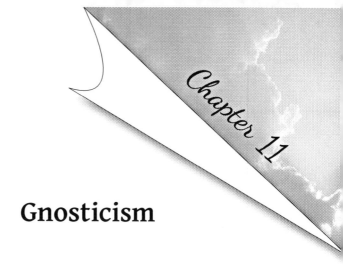

Gnosticism

In Gnostic theologies, heavenly ascents are considered to be a means for believers to find redemption. According to non-canonical Gnostic Christianity (i.e., Gnosticism that is not included in the Protestant or Catholic versions of the Bible), Jesus Christ undertook a journey to heaven and defeated the planetary spirits (archons), thereby enabling his followers to undertake similar journeys. Examples can be found in the texts discovered at Nag Hammadi and the *Pistis Sophia* (a Gnostic text dating back to the third or fourth Century CE), where the Gnostic is rescued from the evil powers and is able to depart from this world through the planetary spheres toward the pleroma, i.e., the abode of the totality of divine powers. The Gnostic text *Pistis Sophia* quotes Christ as saying:

> I flew to the height ... And the gates of the firmament ... all opened at the same time. And all the archons and all the powers and all the angels therein ... looked upon the shining garment of light which I wore, they saw the mystery of their name within it ... saying: "How has the Lord of the All passed through without our knowing?" And all their bonds were loosened, and their places and their ranks.[77]

Similarly, Paul exhorts believers to spiritual warfare:

> For our struggle is not against enemies of blood and
> flesh, but against the rulers, against the authorities,
> against the cosmic powers of this present darkness,
> against the spiritual forces of evil in the heavenly
> places. (Ephesians 6:12)

The above is one of the passages where the apostle seems to use
Gnostic terminology to refer to planetary archons.

> What would that have profited him—to enter
> Paradise or the third heaven—if all these are under
> the realm of the Demiurge, yet, as some would hold,
> he was a participant in mysteries they say are above
> the Demiurge?[78]

Of the two non-canonical Apocalypses inspired by Paul, one
is Gnostic and part of the *Nag Hammadi Codex* V, 2.5., while the
other is Coptic Christian. The writings of the historical Paul on
the third heaven (2 Cor. 12:4.) are substituted with a Gnostic Paul,
who overcomes the unsympathetic Demiurge figure of the seventh
heaven by means of a secret sign (Apoc. Paul 23:25–26) and reaches
the highest, tenth heaven. The Coptic Christian Apocalypse of Paul
envisages a soul-body separation immediately after death and a
physical resurrection at the eschaton, while the Gnostic Apocalypse
separates the souls of the righteous from their bodies permanently,
upon death.

In *The Gnostic Paul*, Elaine Pagels, religious historian and
professor of religion at Princeton University, examines the way in
which Paul's letters in the New Testament can be interpreted either
antignostically, or gnostically. Although ecclesiastical tradition since
the time of Irenaeus has directed interpretation toward an orthodox
exegesis,[79] the Naasenes and Valentinians revered Paul as a Gnostic

initiate, claiming that his receiving of the gnosis was a symbolic one, as set out in the Treatise on the Resurrection, which was discovered at Nag Hammadi:[80]

> The saviour has swallowed up death, so that you should not remain in ignorance (i.e., "death") … and he has offered us the way of our immortality. Therefore, as the Apostle says, we suffered with him, and we arose with him, and we went to heaven with him.[81]

According to Harrison, Paul's revelation is a paradigm for the Gnostic believer's ascent.[82] Furthermore, the motif of the heavenly journey can be seen in John 3:-121. "Jesus replied, '… unless a person is born from above, he cannot see the kingdom of God.'" The phrase "born from above" has been translated as "born again" in the King James Version of the Bible. However, it can also be translated, perhaps more accurately, as "born from heaven" or "born from a higher place." This indicates the pattern of a heavenly journey that we have already encountered. Tertullian, an early Christian writer from Carthage 160 CE–c. 225, argues against those who claim that Paul was a Gnostic, which suggests that this controversy was a serious contention at the time.[83]

Chapter 12

The Book of Revelation and the Kingdom of Heaven

The *Book of Revelation* follows the Jewish apocalyptic traditions, and in it, John records that he sees "there in heaven a door stood open," while an angel tells him to "come up here" (Rev. 4:1–2). John depicts thousands of Jewish elders and countless others belonging to every nation, around God's throne. *Revelation* mainly focuses on the way in which the powers of darkness in the world will be overthrown. The heavenly court described by John is a combination of Hellenistic-Roman ceremony with early Christian worship in a synagogue-like setting. "Just as the celestial liturgy described by John replicates Christian worship or imperial court life, heaven is a sacred space resembling first-century ritual architecture."[84] Biblical scholars and writers McDannell and Lang have classified the views of heaven into two types, namely, theocentric or anthropocentric. A theocentric view of heaven views eternal life as consisting of an immediate experience of God, whereas an anthropocentric viewing comprises pure relationships with others, especially with friends and family. John's visions can be classified as a theocentric heaven, with God and Christ in the center. His New Jerusalem is essentially a temple for full communion with God affirming that seeing God "face to face" is the privilege of those in heaven.

Tertullian, (c. 155–c.240 CE), an important early Christian

theologian, explains that in the eschaton, the heavenly kingdom can be enjoyed when the righteous are changed into angelic bodies:

> When the resurrection of the saints is completed, the destruction of the world and the conflagration of judgment will be effected, we shall be "changed in a moment" into angelic substance, by the "putting on of incorruption" (1 Cor. 15:52-3), and we shall be transferred to the heavenly kingdom.[85]

The millennium refers to God's earthly reign lasting for a thousand years, during which time evil is eliminated from the earth. Believers are raised to heaven after they have enjoyed the pleasures of the earthly paradise. The "Lord's Prayer" (Matthew 6:9–13) begins with "Our Father in heaven" and continues "your will be done, on earth as it is in heaven," implying that the celestial realm is subject to God's will, but his kingdom is yet to come fully to earth. The concept of the coming kingdom of God, instituting heavenly conditions on earth, is of great significance in Christianity. Poythress distinguishes four "levels of communication" in *Revelation*: the words used in the passage; what is seen in the vision; persons or objects that the elements in the vision refer to; and the symbolic significance of the imagery in the vision: word, vision, object, and symbolism levels.[86] John sees the New Jerusalem as "coming down out of heaven from God, prepared as a bride adorned for her husband" (Rev. 21:2). The city may be considered as a symbol for the redeemed in their future glory. Its description as a golden cube city with large pearl gates, guarded by angels and twelve precious foundation stones, is generally not to be taken literally, but more as a model for renewal. The term used for "new" (*kainos*) connotes newness in quality or nature, in contrast with the Greek words *neos,* with the latter connoting newness in time. Similarly, Bede[87] records a layered approach to the interpretation of the Bible, while Solomon literally builds a temple.

Allegorically, it is Christ's body or church; topologically, it is each of the faithful; and analogically, it is the joys of the heavenly mansion.[88]

Christopher Morse, professor of theology and ethics, considers the idea of heaven as the direction from which God acts in relation to earth. God is not confined to heaven, as "Even heaven and the highest heaven cannot contain you" (1 Kings 8:27). When it is said that Christians wait for a "new heaven and a new earth," it refers to God taking a new course of action. Furthermore, earth can be understood through the duality of heaven. Heaven may also be considered as a community where God resides with the angels or seen as a kingdom at hand, not restricted to an upper world or afterlife but even in the present during the daily events of this earth. Jesus likens the kingdom of heaven to such ordinary realities as the sowing of seeds, a grain of mustard seed, leavening in bread, treasure hidden in a field, a pearl, or a wedding feast. On this basis, Morse argues that we are led to conclude that the word *heaven* refers primarily to the current conditions under which we lead our lives.[89]

The Book of Life
Both Jewish and Christian traditions include reference to a heavenly book or scroll, which contains divine decrees and knowledge of human destiny, including future events. The Book of Life (Hebrew *Sefer HaChaim*) is the book in which God records the names of every person who is destined for heaven. According to the Talmud, the Book of Life is opened on Rosh Hashanah, the first day of the Jewish year. In this tradition, God sits in judgment over his creatures and has the Book of Life together with the books containing the records of the righteous and the wicked. The Mishnah states that the actions of every human being are recorded in a book (*Abot,* ii. 1; see iii. 16). The book may be identified with the mysterious book that Moses mentions in Exodus 32:32: "But now, please forgive their sin—but if not, then blot me out of the book you have written". Each person's problems are also recorded in the book, or scroll:

Record my misery;

List my tears on your scroll—

Are they not in your record? (Psalm 56:8, English Standard Version)

In another example, Ezekiel received his commission as a prophet through ingesting a mystical scroll that miraculously appears to him. Shortly thereafter that he is reportedly transported by a heavenly chariot:

> Then the spirit lifted me up, and as the glory of the LORD rose from its place, I heard behind me the sound of loud rumbling; it was the sound of the wings of the living creatures brushing against one another, and the sound of the wheels beside them, that sounded like a loud rumbling. The spirit lifted me up and bore me away. (Ezekiel, 3:12–14)

Similarly, Zechariah has a vision of a flying scroll that delivers fated events across the earth according to divine justice (Zechariah 5:1–3).

In the book of Daniel, those whose names are recorded in the book and who shall escape the troubles preparatory to the coming of the Messianic kingdom are destined to share in everlasting life.

> There shall be a time of anguish, such as has never occurred since nations first came into existence. But at that time your people shall be delivered, everyone who is found written in the book. (Daniel 12:1)

Similarly, in the book of Revelation, a series of predestined events are released in the world by a figure representing Christ ("the

Lamb"), who takes a scroll from the hand of God and opens its seven seals. Also in Revelation, John says that only those whose names are written in the Book of Life are permitted entrance into Jerusalem, or the heavenly city. In Revelation 3:5, the message to the church of Sardis states, "If you conquer, you will be clothed like them in white robes, and I will not blot your name out of the book of life."

> At the final Judgment, "And I saw the dead, great and small, standing before the throne, and books were opened. Also another book was opened, the book of life. And the dead were judged according to their works, as recorded in the books." (Revelation 20:12.)

Each soul is shown as being accountable for its deeds, as recorded in the spiritual book or books of life. Parallels could be drawn between these divine books and what has become known as "the Akashic Records," which concept was introduced by theosophy and anthroposophy (i.e., that events on earth as recorded on an etheric plane of existence). The idea of an akashic record is attributed to Alfred Percy Sinnett, who, in his book *Esoteric Buddhism* (1883), wrote about a Buddhist belief in permanent records in the akasa and the potential of man to read them. C. W. Leadbeater, in his book *Clairvoyance* (1899), identified the akashic records as readable by a clairvoyant.

The concept of a heavenly Book of Life may originate in Babylon.[90] The Babylonian legends refer to the Tablet of Destinies, as well as tablets of wrongdoings. The Tablet of Destinies conferred upon the chief god in the Babylonian pantheon, Enlil, his supreme authority to rule the affairs of humans and gods. The tablet was described as the link between heaven and the underworld.[91]

The Psalmist says:

Then I said, "Here I am;
in the scroll of the book it is written of me.
I delight to do your will, O my God;
your law is within my heart." (Psalm 40:7–8)

Psalm 40 beautifully establishes a connection between what may be written in the divine Book of Life described as "the scroll" and the deep desire of the Psalmist to do God's will based on his sense of divine law being inscribed on his heart. This could be seen as a suggestion that the source of a person's destiny is contained within each one's heart, echoing the later Hermetic maxim "as above, so below."

Chapter 13

The Christian Nicene Creed

The Nicene Creed, also known as the Niceno-Constantinopolitan Creed, is a Christian statement of faith. It is the only ecumenical creed accepted as an authoritative one by the Roman Catholic, Eastern Orthodox, Anglican, and major Protestant churches (*Catechism*, 195). The Nicene Creed was probably issued by the Council of Constantinople held in 381, based on a baptismal creed already in existence. "We believe" is an essential part of the Catechism of the Catholic Church, synthesizing the essential contents of doctrine (*Catechism*, 11). This Ecumenical Council enlarged parts of the original Nicene Creed; for example, concerning the Holy Spirit,[92] condemned several heresies (Arianism, Macedonianism, and Apollinarianism) and made decisions concerning Bishops.[93]

The Nicene Creed

We believe in one God, the Father, the Almighty,
maker of *heaven and earth,*
of all that is, seen and unseen.
We believe in one Lord, Jesus Christ,
the only Son of God, eternally begotten of the Father,
God from God, Light from Light, true God from true God,

begotten, not made, of one Being with the Father.
Through him all things were made.
For us men and for our salvation, *he came down
from heaven*:
by the power of the Holy Spirit he was born of the
Virgin Mary, and became man.
For our sake he was crucified under Pontius Pilate;
he suffered died and was buried.
On the third day he rose again in fulfilment of the
Scriptures;
he ascended into heaven and is seated at the right
hand of the Father.
He will come again in glory to judge the living and
the dead,
and his kingdom will have no end.

We believe in the Holy Spirit, the Lord, the giver
of life,
who proceeds from the Father and the Son.
With the Father and the Son he is worshipped and
glorified.
He has spoken through the Prophets.
We believe in one holy catholic and apostolic
Church.
We acknowledge one baptism for the forgiveness
of sins.
We look for the resurrection of the dead,
and the life of the world to come.
Amen.
(*Catechism*, The Credo)

The creed is an essential summary of Christian beliefs. The word
heaven is mentioned three times in the creed (italics added) and
is pivotal in that it addresses the relationship between God and

Jesus in heaven above and man on earth below, with the resolution of the two in the eschaton after the resurrection. The expression "heaven and earth" means creation in its entirety, indicating the bond uniting heaven and earth, and it distinguishes the one from the other: "the earth" is the world of humanity, whereas "heaven" or "the heavens" can designate both the firmament and God's own "place"— and, consequently, the "heaven," which is eschatological glory. In addition, "heaven" refers to the saints and the place where angels live (*Catechism*, 326). The Catholic Church maintains that through his life, death, and resurrection, Jesus Christ opened heaven to believers, constituting the community of all who are incorporated into Christ. "Looking for" the resurrection of the dead and the life of the world to come is, perhaps, phrased more as a hope than a belief in the Creed. This communion is referred to in scripture by the following images: life, light, peace, wedding feast, wine of the kingdom, the Father's house, and the heavenly Jerusalem, paradise. Yet, it ultimately defies description as "no eye has seen, nor ear heard, nor the heart of man conceived, what God has prepared for those who love him" (*Catechism*, 125–127). According to McGrath, whenever the divine liturgy is celebrated on earth, the boundaries between heaven and earth are removed with earthly worshipers joining in the eternal heavenly liturgy chanted by angels "worshipers have the opportunity of being mystically transported to the threshold of heaven."[94]

According to Rowan Williams, the 104th Archbishop of Canterbury, "eternity is above all a joy in the sheer reality of God— not an absorption in some final 'absolute' but a living relation ... set in the heart of the exchange of life and joy within the Trinity."[95] He cites Augustine who wrote the following about heaven:

> We shall rest and we shall see, we shall see and we shall love, we shall love and we shall praise. Behold what will be at the end without end. For what other end do we have, if not to reach the kingdom which has no end?[96]

Activities

If you have access to a church or cathedral, you could visit and see whether there are depictions of the heavenly realm, whether in pictures or stained-glass windows. Have your ideas of heaven been affected by the traditional images that you have seen in churches, or in books containing photos of cathedrals with their amazing windows?

Chapter 14

Discussion and Conclusions

Now, we near the conclusion of our journey through the different traditions concerning heaven by comparing and contrasting the structure of the cosmos; the nature of the soul; the soul's journey; and the role of morality. The questions we first posed are also addressed and conclusions are reached.

Structure of the Cosmos

A tripartite model is perceived in the cosmologies examined: the heavenly abode of the gods, situated in the sky above; the earth, home of humankind, as the middle realm; and the underworld below, where spirits or the deceased dwell. The soul flight of the shaman is an early example of soul flight of exceptional individuals to heaven, as well as to the middle and lower worlds. The ancient Egyptian cosmos also comprises three main parts: the land of the living, the sky, and the Duat—the otherworld or the underworld, which is usually imagined as lying beneath the earth, but sometimes inside the sky. The dead may reside in the kingdom of Osiris within the Duat, travel with the sun and his boat, or they might live in the pastoral paradise, known as the Field of Reeds.

In Mesopotamia, the universe has a tripartite structure, including multiple levels of heaven. According to Heimpel,[97] at night, the setting sun enters the heavens' interior, where a white house is located and where the moon also resides during times of invisibility.[98] The floor of each of the three layers of heavens is made of stone in different colors. The gods in heaven are organized in the form of an earthly kingdom, including a king at the head of a council with a group of royal functionaries assisting him. There is a Sumerian earthly paradise in the land of Dilmun, normally reserved for gods. In ancient Persia, it was believed that a bridge gave the worthy access to heaven, while other souls would fall off, down into the joyless subterranean kingdom of the dead. However, in Zoroastrianism, this was later replaced by the concept of the last judgment. By the early centuries CE, Zoroastrians believed in the concept of different levels of heaven corresponding to stars and the luminaries, where blessed souls of the deceased resided.

According to Greeks in the Homeric Age, the living dwelt on the earth; the dead resided in Hades; and the gods dwelt on Mt. Olympus. Plato described the earth as a sphere around which revolved the planetary spheres and the fixed stars. Above the heavens, the soul could contemplate eternal verities in the realm of the Absolute.

According to the Jewish perspective in the Hebrew Bible, the primal duality is between above and below, with heaven being the first in creation. The ancient Israelites perceived the cosmos as comprising a tripartite structure: heaven or sky (*shamayim*) above, earth (*eres*) in the middle, and the netherworld (*sheol*) below. The heavenly realm was perceived to be vast like a cosmic canopy or "firmament," with a floor of precious stone (Isa. 40:12, 55:9). God (Yahweh) is a mighty celestial king, ruling over the world and over an assembly of heavenly beings. They believed in a clear dualism of heaven and hell, with heaven being multilayered. According to Hekhalot and Merkabah mysticism, God travels through the heavenly realms, either in a chariot or in a celestial palace. "Abraham's Bosom" represents an intermediate realm where the righteous may rest before entering into heaven proper.

Elements of the Jewish tradition of multiple heavens were passed on to Christianity; for example, the apostle Paul records that he ascended to the third heaven. The Hebrew and Greek words for heaven, *shamayim* and *ouranus,* have been distinctly used in the Bible: The sky of air, clouds and rain, where birds fly (Gen.1:20, 26, 28; 8:2; Deut. 28:12, Ps. 147:8; Matt. 8:20; 13:32; 16:2–3); space as the physical "heavens" of the sun, moon and stars (Gen 1:14, 15,17; 15:5; Deut. 4:19; 28:62; Acts 2:19–20; Heb. 11:12); and the spiritual realm, where God and the angels dwell.

Christianity retains the Jewish view of heaven being God's abode. The Lord's Prayer (Matthew 6:9–13) begins with "Our Father in heaven," being the primary address to the deity. It continues, "Your kingdom come, Your will be done, on earth as it is in heaven." This implies that the celestial realm is subject to God's will and the coming kingdom of God, which would institute heavenly conditions on earth. The book of Revelation prophesies the coming eschaton in symbolic terms, describing the New Jerusalem descending to earth like a bride adorned for her husband, while describing the dimensions of the city in physical terms. In contrast, statements such as, "Repent, for the kingdom of heaven has come near" (Matt. 3:2) could suggest that heaven refers to the current conditions under which our life is really being lived[99]—where the believer experiences a sense of connection with the divine. At the same time, heaven is conceived of as an eternity of the believer's soul abiding in God's love. This resembles Platonism, where the soul travels to an ethereal realm to contemplate on the divine. Christianity thus incorporates the structure of Jewish cosmology, offering a transcendent experience of the divine similar to Plato and additionally expects the eventual establishment of heaven on earth.

The Nature of the Soul

Shamanism is a paradigm for understanding disparate cultural practices, where the spirit of the practitioner is believed to detach itself from the body to navigate other levels of reality, interact with the spirits therein, and return to the body with increased power or knowledge.

The ancient Egyptian view of the human being is complex: the part of the individual known as the *Ka* is usually translated as spirit, image, or vital force. It can appear as a duplicate of the person, the vital force that continues after death, while the *Ba* or soul in the image of a bird with a human head separates itself from the body at the time of death. The *Ka* needs to be sustained with funerary offerings but can also subsist on wall paintings of food offerings.[100] Gordon, in his definition of the *Ka*, states that while the vital force leaves the deceased at death, it must rejoin the deceased in the afterlife. It may be identified with the Hebrew *ruach* or *nephesh*, the life-spirit.[101] Zabkar disputes the dualistic view of the body being divided into the corpse and *Ankh, Ka,* or *Ba*, saying that both remain connected in Egyptian thought.[102] Hence, the phrase "*Ba* to heaven" may express the wish that the *Ba* may enjoy freedom of movement in the heavenly realms without being limited to it. After an efficacious ritual is performed, the individual is "risen and made whole" and enters upon a new glorified life, conceived of in physical terms. On the other hand, according to Smith, the ancient Egyptian concept of the human being comprises a corporeal self and a social self[103] with Osiris providing a model for resurrection and restoration.

The ability of the human soul to gain immortality after death in the presence of the gods, whether in the celestial realm or the paradisiacal Field of Reeds, depended on a highly ritualized and complex process for the privileged in ancient Egypt. In ancient Mesopotamia, the vast majority of deceased subsisted as ghosts in the underworld, lacking vitality and dependent on the ritual offerings of their living descendants. A similar situation prevailed in ancient Persia, although, in Zoroastrianism, it was believed that the physical body would be resurrected and reunited with the soul in heaven as an interim stage, until after the last judgment, when the gods would confer immortality on the resurrected bodies of the blessed.

The Greeks believed that the soul experiences immortality when separated from the mortal body. After the cycle of birth and death, in addition to rewards and punishments in the hereafter, the soul would regain its purity and return to its star in the Empyrean.

Orthodox Christianity shares a belief in physical resurrection, in common with Judaism and Zoroastrianism. There is no clear indication regarding the religion that first proposed the belief. While there is no proven historical connection, it seems likely, as Barr observed, that there were mutual influences among the traditions, including themes such as resurrection and the last judgment, which people may have understood differently in different cultural contexts.[104] Indeed, it is a general observation that although some common elements emerge among the different traditions, each has a unique frame of reference.

During the intermediate state between death and the final judgment and resurrection, the soul may rest in Abraham's Bosom or Paradise. The righteous "become as angels" and are not given in marriage in heaven like regular human beings on earth. The *Angelic Liturgy* could support the concept that a process of angelification was envisaged among the priests at Qumran. This concept is built on a Hebrew tradition that one greatly favored by God may rarely be taken up to heaven and transformed into an angel, as Enoch was transformed into Metatron. Himmelfarb concludes her considerations of ascent to heaven in Jewish and Christian apocalypses by surmising that they suggest an understanding of human possibility, of the status of the righteous in the universe that goes beyond anything found in the Bible. According to her, ancient Jews and Christians could imagine themselves being as glorious as Enoch, in the midst of their unsatisfactory daily lives. Her conclusion may be correct with respect to the Hebrew Bible, but angelomorphism is an integral part of the Christian biblical tradition, having received much attention. Followers of Jesus Christ believe that they will benefit from the process of resurrection in a perfectly angelic body, by being united with him spiritually. The concept of the faithful serving God in heaven in the form of divinely appointed priests finds a resonance with the figure of Melchizedek in the Old Testament and the Order of Melchizedek, with Christ as the High Priest referred to by Paul, the apostle. This belief is built on the Jewish tradition of the mystical heavenly temple, visited by Merkabah and Hekalot practitioners. Gnostics seek the liberation of the soul from the enslaving material world, believing that Jesus had "risen" only in a spiritual sense. Some elements of Christian scripture can be subject to both orthodox and Gnostic exegeses.[105] For example, Paul's epistles could be perceived as speaking symbolically of receiving gnosis or bodily resurrection.

The Soul's Journey

Shamanic initiation allows the soul to ascend via a ladder or pole (*axis mundi*), assisted by spirits or even psychoactive substances, in search of power or knowledge. The Mesopotamian view did not envisage human beings making such an ascent to heavenly realms, except in exceptional circumstances. However, priests could enter God's presence by worshiping him in elevated Ziggurats or temples.

In ancient Egypt, the appropriate magical procedures were required for navigating a complex topography and guarded portals in the afterlife to gain an opportunity for immortality, perhaps involving visionary shamanic flight for priestly initiates while still alive.

According to Jewish beliefs, Sheol was the destination of the deceased, although the concept of a more beneficial post-mortem destination developed over time, where the righteous deceased would await final judgement in the coming Messianic era and resurrection of the body. Merkabah and Hekalot literature describes visionary ascents in the heavenly realms by remarkable sages possessing the required magical knowledge and moral qualities for gaining wisdom and proximity to God.

In Plato's *Myth of Er*, the hero witnesses souls being rewarded or punished, according to their behavior on earth, in heaven, or in Tartarus, including through metempsychosis. A similar journey is recorded in Zoroastrian literature, in the *Book of Arda Viraf*, aided by a narcotic draught. However, once the soul is pure enough, it can return to its destined star in the empyrean realm to enjoy immortality and divine verities. In a pattern of visionary journeys, the Mysteries of Mithras, in so far as they are known, provide a schematic whereby initiates can experience a heavenly journey, by ascending through the planetary spheres and returning to earth in preparation for their eventual post-mortem journey. As there were seven grades of initiation, perhaps special passwords, gestures, or other secret knowledge allowed them to navigate progressively higher realms associated with the planetary spheres.

The Gnostics believed that the souls of the deceased would try to rise through the planetary spheres but that without the aid of Jesus Christ, they would be unable to pass the hostile planetary powers seeking to limit the aspirant to the lower realms. However, as Christ had overcome the archons, he would aid the believers in achieving liberation from the evil material world and enter the heavenly realm of the spirit.

Christianity makes Jesus Christ central to the believer's heavenly journey. In case of the righteous, there is an intermediate rest in Abraham's Bosom or paradise, followed by a final resurrection on judgment day when each person receives a new body similar to that of an angel, with the kingdom of God being fully established on earth. The doctrine of metempsychosis was rejected with the emphasis being on "salvation by grace through faith" and not on individual effort. (Eph. 2:8: "For by grace you have been saved through faith, and this not your own doing; it is the gift of God.") Thus, the technology of magic, recitations, overcoming of archons, or navigation of planetary spheres in the after world were no longer necessary, as required by the ancient Egyptians, Merkabah traditions of Judaism and the Gnostics and nor were the ancestral initiations or spirit guides of the traditional shaman. It is believed that Jesus declared these measures irrelevant to reaching the most exalted levels of existence: "Jesus answered, 'I am the way and the truth and the life. No one comes to the Father except through me'" (John 14:6). Christianity conceives the idea of becoming a child of God and entering into a loving relationship with him. Those who do not accept God's grace, however, are not accepted into heaven and are destined for darkness and torment. The Zoroastrian view is that there is no Messiah figure to assist believers in the transition at the eschaton.

Relevance of Morality

Moral judgments determine the events in one's afterlife: in ancient Egypt, the heart of the deceased was weighed before the gods to determine its worthiness for immortality, in addition to magical mastery. In Mesopotamia, the future of the deceased in the underworld is decided by the sun, who, after setting, functions as "judge of those above and below."[106] A moral dimension can also be found in Zoroastrianism, in which a tribunal of gods weigh the soul's thoughts and deeds to declare it as worthy of Paradise. This is followed by the day of judgment, after which the righteous are resurrected and rewarded with joyful immortality.

In ancient Greece, the souls of the deceased were judged on the condition of their souls and sent either to paradise on the Isle of the Blessed or to torment in Tartarus. Later, souls return to earth through transmigration, eventually achieving a place in the Empyrean heaven. The Mysteries of Mithras trained Roman initiates to make the heavenly journey through the planetary spheres that they would traverse after death, based on knowledge transmitted in secret ceremonies. As most men were serving military and administrative officers, civil virtues were likely to be important for gaining admission to the cult.

The God of the Jewish Bible, Jehovah or Yahweh (translated from the Hebrew YHVH), in biblical texts, is a king, ruler, and judge (Isa. 33:22), and it is essential to follow God's laws for a positive outcome in the final conclusion of the divine plan. In the Merkabah Jewish tradition, the possession of moral qualities is a precondition for being admitted to gain knowledge of theosophical doctrines and principles, including the knowledge of secret passwords and magical techniques.

While Jews and Christians worship Jehovah, only Christians place faith in Jesus Christ as the Messiah for forgiveness of sins, thereby allowing access to heaven. In *Apologeticus*, Tertullian defends the Christian belief regarding post-mortem judgment in the face of pagan (Graeco-Roman) criticisms, at the same time revealing similarities between the two traditions:

> We are also ridiculed because we proclaim that God is going to judge the world. Yet even the poets and philosophers place a judgment seat in the underworld. In the same way, if we threaten Gehenna, which is a store of hidden underground fire for purposes of punishment, we are received with howls of derision. Yet, they, likewise, have the river Pyriphlegethon in the place of the dead. And if we mention paradise, a place of divine delight appointed to receive the spirits of the saints ... then the Elysian Fields have anticipated the faith.[107]

Conclusions

We have considered the conduct or conditions believed to be necessary for a human being to enter the heavenly realms and whether such concepts emphasize the importance of faith in the divine, require personal moral responsibility, and/or point to special knowledge of magical techniques for attaining heavenly realms. Other questions for which we sought answers are: What elements of older religious beliefs and practices are found in Christianity? What is the perceived relationship between heaven and earth? What are the most important aspects of concepts of heaven?

Of the concepts of heaven found in ancient Egypt, Mesopotamia, Persia, Rome, and Greece, some correspond with those of Judaism and Christianity, where heaven signifies eternal rest, plenty, and joy for the virtuous deceased. The earlier concepts of heaven tended to emphasize descriptions of the heavenly realm as a fertile garden or plain with abundant water and clement weather, such as the Elysian Fields and the Field of Reeds of ancient Egypt, in which the deceased could pursue diverting and pleasant pastimes. While the garden of Eden was an early model of paradise for Christians, later Christian concepts became increasingly abstract, incorporating elements of the temple tradition of Judaism and perhaps influenced by Platonic thought of a hereafter for the blessed in the Empyrean heaven, until it incorporated both life on earth and an eternity with God that defies description. All cosmologies are oriented around a three-tiered view of the world, including a lower world initially for the deceased, the middle realm of the living on earth, and the upper heavenly realms of the gods, to which human beings aspire. Underlying this triplicity is the basic duality of above and below. Christianity hopes for the overcoming of this duality with the establishment of the kingdom of heaven on earth at the conclusion of god's plan for the earth, the Eschaton, and linked to this is the idea of transformation of the whole human being into a citizen of that kingdom.

Admission to the heavenly realms is conditional on meeting certain moral criteria, which varied between the traditions examined. In ancient Egypt and some subsequent mystical Jewish and Gnostic traditions, knowledge of magical procedures was believed to have been an important requirement. These technical magical requirements had the disadvantage of being time-consuming and requiring education, which was not available to the general populace; or in the case of Greece, they anticipated lengthy purification of the soul in the afterlife and metempsychosis; while in Rome observing civic duties appeared to secure a beneficial afterlife. Judaism does not strongly emphasize post-mortem experiences in the afterlife but rather looks forward to the resurrection of the righteous in the Messianic era. However, the development of a sense of dualism, with divine judgment applied to the individual in Judaism, with an increasing dualism in concepts of the afterlife—where a soul could be consigned to Gehenna (hell) or Abraham's Bosom (heavenly paradise) was carried through into Christianity. Christianity rejects metempsychosis and emphasizes faith in Jesus Christ, who enables believers to overcome the limitations (or sins) that would otherwise disqualify them from entering heaven. Gnosticism shares much with early Christianity but differs in the ideas pertaining to salvation through knowledge rather than faith and its focus on the evils of the material world, the demi-god (or demiurge) that created it, and wrathful supernatural beings. Gnostics reject the concept of bodily resurrection, which is shared by Christianity, Judaism, and Zoroastrianism, along with the importance of the mummified physical body in Egypt; and the ancient Greeks also denied the importance of the physical body in the afterlife. The writings of Paul the apostle show the ways in which the interpretations of the early Christian narrative can be interpreted in different ways (e.g., orthodox versus gnostic). Comparing Paul's ministry with elements of shamanism enables the understanding of his work as a "spirit master" from a wider perspective. The pattern of journeying from earth into the heavenly realms with the aid of spirits, whether ancestors, angels, or other entities, to gain power and wisdom is found in shamanism and paralleled in various ways in the traditions examined. Overall, especially in the later cosmologies, there is a shared perception that the universe is moral at its core, and that people will be rewarded or punished in the afterlife based on their actions and intentions while alive. The magical techniques applied by some traditions are largely a way to accelerate or facilitate access to the heavenly realms but do not completely replace the necessity of being morally worthy in terms of the values of those respective cultures.

Another element that is important to gaining access to the heavenly realms emerges from the later Western religions (i.e., that of the transformation of the individual undertaking the journey in the afterlife). The process for each qualified soul to enter heaven resulted in the transformation of a mortal being into an immortal.

It was hoped that this process would rectify the disruption caused by death to the constitution of the individual and his/her social world. Biblical Christianity expects—or "looks for" in terms of the Nicene Creed regarding the resurrection—a radical transformation of the individual into a heavenly being comparable to an angel. With that lofty status—the term *angel* arising from the Greek *aggelos,* meaning messenger—the individual is able to act in ways more closely aligned with God's purposes. According to one line of tradition, as foreshadowed in the *Angelic Liturgy* as well as the *Enoch* Apocalypses and further elaborated by the apostle Paul and other New Testament writers, the individual may eventually serve as a kind of priest in the heavenly sanctuary, following the pattern set by Christ as High Priest in the order of Melchizedek (i.e., a non-hereditary priesthood role based on selection by God). The individual thus achieves not only the freedom from toil promised by afterlife worldly paradises in the Western religious traditions, but also an elevated station in life eternal and acknowledgment of his or her personal value in heaven based on his or her relationship with God.

In identifying the important aspects of heaven, McDannell and Lang classified views of heaven as either theocentric (centered on God) or anthropocentric (centered on human beings). Elements of community and worship of deities were present in most traditions with, perhaps, more emphasis on the theocentric in Christianity. However, as indicated in the Episcopal think tank referred to in Chapter 1, it is important for believers to expect to be reunited with loved ones in the hereafter, along with the doctrine of the Communion of the Saints (*communo sanctorum,* a fellowship of, or with, the saints) in some denominations.[108]

Concepts of heaven and earth place these realms as being located far apart—as a reflection of the primary duality of "above" and "below," or of sky and earth. With the sky as the abode of the high gods and the chief God as divine king ruling over the heavenly host and life on earth, "above" and heaven was seen as the direction from which divine authority was wielded. With the Ptolemaic worldview and the planetary spheres around the earth, people were still influenced by the astronomical and astrological influences emanating from above. Furthermore, Babylonian divination practices aimed to learn the will of the gods mainly by observing signs and activities in the sky. Likewise, Ra was a powerful god bringing light to earth from his heavenly boat, with other sky gods also playing an important role in ancient Egypt. In Christianity, the Nicene Creed encapsulates the view that Christ ascended from earth to heaven, where he sits on the right hand of God the Father and from where he will judge the living and the dead. From the earliest temple traditions, approaches to the gods through worship have resulted in a separation of the sacred from the profane through entering sacred space, with this being mirrored in views of the soul's journey in the afterlife being progressively from the profane to the sacred.

However, other aspects of Christianity have brought heaven and earth closer together, with the expectation of the kingdom of heaven being established on earth—and before that, heavenly experiences are possible for believers on earth through worship and community. As a consequence, earth and heaven, as well as hell and purgatory, can be seen increasingly as part of a continuum of experience, rather than as entirely separate.

The cosmologies that we have examined emphasize that if individuals make choices that align with authentic values of their society during the course of their lives (i.e., by choosing "the good") and by worshiping the deity or deities possessing the power of bestowing transcendence of earthly time, then they can expect to achieve immortality along with other benefits, such as communion with the divine. One result of the transference from the "lower" to the "higher" part of the continuum of life would be to experience life more as a denizen of the heavenly realms was imagined to be experienced (i.e., to become more "angelic"). Meditative prayer practices could further prepare the individual for entering a paradisiacal experience of life. In this way, heaven becomes less a physical location in the sky, but rather an orientation toward the sacred in life. The dichotomy between heaven and earth, "above" and "below," depends on the perspective and orientation of the person perceiving them. Life on earth includes experiences corresponding to periods of elevated awareness and therefore, by analogy, closer to the heavenly powers. Similarly, life on earth may be perceived of as not completely disconnected from the hereafter but rather as shaped by the thoughts and actions of individuals, which influence conditions while alive, as well as those that are desired or imagined in the afterlife. Therefore, the concept of heaven should not be regarded just as an iconic focus for the imagination, as McGrath suggested,[109] or solely the beatific vision and the mystical union and Russell stated,[110] but as part of an active process of engagement by the individual in the context of their expectations for the future, including the afterlife.

Activity
This is an exercise in active imagination, or journeying, whereby we can experience aspects of the imaginal realms by engaging our own imagination intentionally.

An Inner Journey to a Chapel

Sit quietly in a private space where you won't be disturbed, including by pets. Mute your phone and dim or switch off your computer and television. You may read and commit to memory the steps in the journey, make your own recording, leaving plenty of time between sentences to experience the scenes, or even ask a sympathetic friend or family member to read it for you. Take some deep breaths and relax. Focus on your breathing for a short time. Have a sense of grounding by imagining silver roots wrapping around your lower calves and feet, and going deep within the earth, until you feel a solid sense of connection with being grounded into the earth.

You are driven in a comfortable car to a beautiful small white wooden church surrounded by a garden and trees in the churchyard.

You get out of the car and enter through a red door into the chapel's small, welcoming lobby, which is fragrant with the aroma of frankincense and flowers. A beautiful vase of flowers with roses and white lilies sits on a low table. There is an attendant at the cloak room, and you hand over to him or her something that you don't need, such as your coat or scarf, so you can enter the chapel unencumbered.

Once inside the chapel proper, you admire the richly colored light filtering through the jewel-like stained-glass windows. You see that different stories from the Bible are shown on the windows: In one, you see angels going up and down the ladder to heaven (Jacob's ladder) as Jacob sleeps below. In another, Ezekiel is riding in his chariot of fire toward heaven, while in yet another window baby Moses is in the rushes being discovered by the daughter of the pharaoh. In another window, you see Jesus depicted dressed in shining white linen robes, welcoming the people who surround him. A large round rose-patterned stained glass window is above the altar, with many vibrant colors making a pattern that reminds you of the beauty and order of life in all its dimensions.

You sit down on one of the wooden pews. Which of the stained-glass windows particularly attracts you? Is it one of those described above, or something different and personal to you? You have the choice to enter through any of the stained-glass windows, each of which is a way to approach the heavenly realms, and experience something of what may be found there.

As you relax, the scene in the window seems to open up into a three-dimensional scene, and you can imagine that you enter it like a doorway. See what you see, hear what you hear, and feel what you feel, as you become aware of your surroundings. A friendly figure might appear before you. If you have any questions about heaven or anything else, you may ask this person, who will respond with what you need to know at this time. Take careful note of what he or she says. They might show you something of relevance to your life.

It is now time to leave, and you feel yourself gently drawn back out of the scene depicted in the window, and into the chapel once again. The window is now two dimensional again, but you carry within you the wisdom of the answer or answers that you just received.

You return to the chapel lobby and collect whatever you left with the attendant, or you may decide to leave it or something else you would like to give to charity. You exit the building, and your driver is waiting for you outside in the sunshine, to bring you safely back home.

Taking deep breaths and moving your toes and fingers, you find yourself safely back in your room, where you may feel like taking a moment to journal about your experience.

Our Return

And our stay among the stars
Has ended for now.
With a fresh view of life,
We softly alight.
Bringing wisdom and gratitude,
We breathe in, we breathe out.
Hand in hand and smiling,
We glance all about
And quietly give thanks to the all.
Thanks for the journey, thanks for the light,
Thanks for the tales that glow ever bright,
Thanks for our insights and love to expand,
Thanks for the heaven we enjoy in this land.

Joann Greig
Pristina, 2017

-The End-

Endnotes

1   Jeffrey Burton Russell, A History of Heaven – The Singing Silence (Princeton, NJ: Princeton University Press, 1997) xiii, xiv.

2   Wolf Liebeschuetz, "The Rise and Fall of the Afterlife. The 1995 Read-Tuckwell Lecture at the University of Bristol by J. N. Bremmer", *Journal of Roman Studies* 94, (2004): 208.

3   Alister E. McGrath, A Brief History of Heaven. (Malden, MA:Wiley-Blackwell, 2003) 166.

4   J. Edward Wright, The Early History of Heaven (New York, NY: Oxford University Press, 2000).

5   Nicholas Campion, The Dawn of Astrology: A Cultural History of Western Astrology, Vol.1: The Ancient and Classical Worlds (London: Continuum Books, 2008), xi.

6   Mary C. Neale, *To Heaven and Back. A Doctor's Extraordinary Account of Her Death, Heaven, Angels, and Life Again: A True Story* (Colorado Springs: WaterBrook Press, 2012).

7   C. Michael Smith, "Jung and Shamanism in Dialogue: Retrieving the soul, Retrieving the Sacred" (2nd ed., Victoria BC, Canada: Trafford Publishing, 2007), 96.

8   I.M. Lewis, *Religion in Context: Cults and Charisma* (2nd ed.; Cambridge: Cambridge University Press, 1996), 105-21.

9   J. Edward Wright, *The Early History of Heaven* (Oxford: Oxford University Press, 2000), ix.

10 Samuel A.B. Mercer, *The Pyramid Texts* (New York: Longmans, Green & Co, 1952) Utterance 572.

11 R. O. Faulker, The Ancient Egyptian Coffin Texts. Vol. 1-III. (Stilwell, KS: Digireads, 1973 (2007).

12 Eva Von Dassow (Ed.), Raymond Faulkner (Trans.), James Wasserman (Foreword), *The Egyptian Book of the Dead: The Book of Going Forth by Day* (San Francisco: Chronicle Books, 1994, 1998, 2008).

13 Nicholas Campion. *The Dawn of Astrology* (London: Continuum, 2008), 94.

14 Zabkar, 62.

[15] See also *Coffin Text* 467.

[16] Taylor, 132.

[17] Wright, *Early History of Heaven*, 115.

[18] Campion, *Dawn of Astrology*, 90.

[19] Edward F. Wente, "Mysticism in Pharaonic Egypt", *Journal of Near Eastern Studies*, Vol. 41, No. 3 (1982): 178-179.

[20] The light of a star or planet when close to the horizon separates into three rays - blue-violet above, green in the middle and red below and perhaps was the basis for the colors of the three heavens. Erica Reiner and David Pingree., *Babylonian Planetary Omens 2*. 1981, 19.

[21] A.L. Oppenheim, "A Babylonian Diviners Manual", *Journal of Near Eastern Studies* 33, (1974): 204.

[22] Morris Jastrow and Albert T. Clay, An Old Babylonian version of the Gilgamesh Epic (New Haven: Yale University Press, 1920), x.ii. 4-5.

[23] Wright, 45.

[24] Mills, L.H. (trans.) "Yasna," in *Sacred Books of the East* (American Edition, 1898), 32.13.

[25] *Yasna*, 331.

[26] R.C. Zaehner, *The Dawn and Twilight of Zoroastrianism* (Whitefish, MT: Literary Licensing, 2011), 302-5.

[27] *Yasna*, 30.7.

[28] E.W. West, (trans.) "Pahlavi Texts," in *Sacred Books of the East* (Oxford: Oxford University Press, 1860) Pahl. Riv. Dd. XL.VIII, 99,100, 107.

[29] Alan F. Segal, Life After Death: A History of the Afterlife in the Religions of the West (New York: Doubleday, 2003), 93.

[30] Martin Haug (trans.) "Book of Arda Viraf," in *Sacred Books and Early Literature of the East, Volume VII: Ancient Persia*, edited by Charles F. Horne (Bombay: Govt. Central Book Depot, 1872, 1917).

[31] Haug, *The Book of Arda Viraf*, 7:1-9.

[32] Kenneth, W. Tupper, "Entheogens and Existential Intelligence: The use of Plant Teachers as Cognitive Tools," *Canadian Journal of Education*, 27, no.4 (2002): 499.

[33] Homer. *The Odyssey*. A.T. Murray (trans.) (Cambridge, MA., Harvard University Press; London, William Heinemann, Ltd. 1919), 11:90.

[34] Such as Ganymedes, who was taken to heaven to "pour drink for the gods in the house of Zeus". *The Homeric Hymns and Homerica*, Hugh G. Evelyn-White (trans) (Cambridge, MA., Harvard University Press; London, William Heinemann Ltd. 1914), 5:200.

[35] Homer, *Odyssey*, 4.561-568.

36   Aristophanes "Peace," in *The Complete Greek Drama*, vol. 2. Eugene O'Neill, Jr. (New York: Random House, 1938), 830-840.

37   Pindar. Odes. Diane Arnson Svarlien (trans). 1990. 2.52-70.

38   Plato. "Timaeus," in Plato in Twelve Volumes, Vol. 9, W.R.M. Lamb (trans.) (Cambridge, MA, Harvard University Press; London, William Heinemann Ltd., 1925), 38c-d.

39   Marjorie O'Rourke Boyle," Pure of Heart: From Ancient Rites to Renaissance Plato", Journal *of the History of Ideas*, Vol. 63, No. 1 (Jan., 2002), 48.

40   Plato, *Phaedrus, 246c7-dl, 247c2-7*.

41   Plato, *Timaeus*, 41d8.

42   Plato, *Gorgias*, 524c-e.

43   Porphyry, *De Antro,*10.

44   Beck, *Mithras Cult*, 106.

45   David Ulansay, *The origins of the Mithraic mysteries: Cosmology and salvation in the ancient world*, (Oxford: Oxford University Press, 1989) 105.

46   Hans Dieter Betz, The Greek Magical Papyri in Translation, including the Demotic Spells, Vol 1. (Chicago: University of Chicago Press, 1992), 48.

47   Walter Scott, Hermetica, Vol. 1: The Ancient Greek and Latin Writings Which Contain Religious or Philosophic Teachings Ascribed to Hermes Trismegistus (Boston, Massachusetts: Shambhala, 1985) Libellus I.25, 129.

48   Franz Cumont, *Astrology and Religion among the Greeks and Romans, American lectures on the history of religions*, series of 1911-1912, New York and London, G. P. Putnam, [1912], 108.

49   3 *Enoch; Synopse,*1; trans. Alexander, 3 Enoch, 255.

50   Abel, 102.

51   J.J. Collins, Apocalypse: Morphology of a Genre (Missoula, MT: Scholars Press,1979), 9.

52   R.H. Charles (ed.) *The Book of the Secrets of Enoch*, W R Morfill (Trans.) Filiquarian Publishing, 2006.

53   Vita Daphna Arbel, *Beholders of Divine Secrets: Mysticism and Myth in the Hekhalot and Merkavah Literature* (New York: State University of New York Press, 2003), 144.

54   Smith, Morton (trans.). *Hekhalot Rabbati: The Greater Treatise concerning the Palaces of Heaven*. Edited by Don Karr, corrected by Gershom Scholem. (Morton Smith Estate: Digital Brilliance, 1943-7 (2009)), Synopse 228.

55   Elior. Rachel. *The Three Temples: On the Emergence of Jewish Mysticism*. David Louvish (trans.) (Portland: Littman Library of Jewish Civilization, 2005), 63.

56 Chapter XLVIII (c), ALT 3 (6).

57 Elliot R. Wolfson, 'Mysticism and the Poetic-Liturgical Compositions from Qumran: A Response to Bilhah Nitzan', *Jewish Quarterly Review, New Series* 85, No. 1/2, Papers on the Dead Sea Scrolls (1994): p. 186.

58 Elliot R. Wolfson, 'Yeridah la-Merkavah: Typology of Ecstasy and Enthronement in Ancient Jewish Mysticism', in *Mystics of the Book: Themes, Topics and Typologies*, ed. R. A. Herrera (New York: Peter Lang Publishing, 1993): 13-44.

59 Elliot R. Wolfson, *Language, Eros, Being: Kabbalistic Hermeneutics and Poetic Imagination* (New York, NY: Fordham University Press, 2005), pp. 120-121.

60 Wolfson, 'Mysticism and the Poetic-Liturgical Compositions from Qumran', p. 193.

61 Wolfson, 'Yeridah la-Merkavah', p. 26.

62 Elliot R. Wolfson, 'Seven Mysteries of Knowledge: Qumran Esotericism Reconsidered', in *The Idea of Biblical Interpretation: Essays in Honor of James L. Kugel*, ed. H. Najman (Leiden: Brill, 2003), p. 192.

63 Jabir ibn Hayyan, 'The Emerald Tablet of Hermes Trismegistus' in Holmyard, E.J., *Alchemy*, (Harmondsworth: Penguin Books, 1957), line 2. http://www.sacred-texts.com/alc/emerald.htm. See also Wolfson, 'Seven Mysteries of Knowledge', p. 192.

64 Himmelfarb, Martha. *Ascent to Heaven in Jewish and Christian Apocalypses*. (New York: Oxford University Press, 1993), 3.

65 G. H. McCurdy, "Platonic Orphism in the Testament of Abraham," *Journal of Biblical Literature*, 61 (1942), 213-15, 221, 226.

66 While the date of this Book is unknown, it could be fairly late i.e. during the Sasanian Dynasty from 224 CE to 651 CE. See Charles Horne, "Ancient Persia" In *The Sacred Books and Early Literature of the East* (New York: Parke, Austin and Lipscomb, 1917) 185. In this case, the writers could well have been influenced by Greek and Jewish traditions.

67 James Barr, "The Question of Religious Influence: The Case of Zoroastrianism, Judaism, and Christianity," *Journal of the American Academy of Religion*, 53, No. 2 (1985): 201-235.

68 Irenaeus. "On the Final Restoration of Creation." In Alister E. McGrath (ed.), *The Christian Theology Reader*, second ed., (Oxford: Blackwell Publishing), 1995 (2001) 611.

69 Tertullian. *Tertullian: Adversus Marcionem*. Ed. and trans. Ernest Evans. (London: Oxford University Press) 1972.

[70] See my article on the topic, "Angelomorphism and Magical Transformation in the Christian and Jewish Traditions", *Celestial Magic, special issue of Culture and Cosmos,* Vol. 19, nos. 1 and 2, 2015, pp. 129-44.

[71] James R. Davila, Liturgical Works: Eerdman's Commentaries on the Dead Sea Scrolls (Michigan: Eerdmans Publishing, 2000), 1.

[72] Crispin Fletcher-Louis. *All the Glory of Adam: Liturgical Anthropology in the Dead Sea Scrolls* (Leiden, E.J. Brill, 2002), 56.

[73] James R. Davila, 'Heavenly Ascents in the Dead Sea Scrolls,' in *Dead Sea Scrolls After Fifty Years, 2* (Leiden: Brill, 1999), pp. 461–85. For the imaginal, see Corbin, Henri, 'Mundus Imaginalis: the Imaginary and the Imaginal', *Spring,* 1972, pp. 1–19 http://www.hermetic.com/bey/mundus_imaginalis.htm

[74] Fletcher-Lewis, *All the Glory of Adam,* 203.

[75] Segal, 306.

[76] Fletcher-Louis, *Luke-Acts,* p. 105; see also Fletcher-Louis, *All the Glory of Adam.*

[77] Meade (trans.), *Pistis Sophia,* [1921], 2005.

[78] Tertullian, "Prescription Against Heretics" 24-30. Translated by Peter Holmes. In *Ante-Nicene Fathers,* Vol. 3. Edited by Alexander Roberts, James Donaldson, and A. Cleveland Coxe. (Buffalo, NY: Christian Literature Publishing Co., 1885.)

[79] Elaine Pagels, The Gnostic Paul – Gnostic Exegesis of the Pauline Letters (New York, NY: Continuum International Publishing Group, 1992), 152.

[80] Pagels, *The Gnostic Paul,* p. 29 with reference to the *Treatise on the Resurrection,* a Gnostic text found at Nag Hammadi sometimes referred to as "The Letter to Rheginos". See Willis Barnstone, ed., *The Gnostic Bible,* 2003. The Treatise on the Resurrection *(Nag Hammadi Codex I, 4)* http://gnosis.org/naghamm/resurrection-barnstone.html (accessed 25 September 2016.)

[81] *Epistula ad Rheginum (De Resurrectione),* Coptic text ed. and trans. M. Malinine, H.Ch. Puech, G. Quispel, W. Till, (Zuerich:Rascher, 1963) 45.14-28 quoted in Pagels, 29 regarding Rom 6:3-4 and Col. 3:4.

[82] J.R. Harrison, "Quest of the Third Heaven: Paul & His Apocalyptic Imitators", *Vigiliae Christianae,* Vol. 58, No. 1 (2004), 24-55, 29.

[83] Tertullian, "Prescription Against Heretics" 30.

[84] McDannell and Lang, *Heaven: A History,* 41.

[85] Tertullian. *Tertullian: Adversus Marcionem.* Edited and translated by Ernest Evans (London: Oxford University Press, 1972), III, 25:6.

[86] Vern Sheridan Poythress, *Journal of the Evangelical Theological Society* 36 (1993): 41-54.

87 Historian of English Christianity c. 672–735.

88 McGrath, *A Brief History of Heaven.*

89 Christopher Morse. *The Difference Heaven Makes: Rehearing the Gospel as News* (London:T&T Clark International, 2010), 24.

90 See Creation Tab. iv. 121, and the Zu legend, ii. 7, quoted in Harper's "Babylonian Legends," in Beitr. z. Assyriologie by Delitzsch and Haupt, 1892, ii. 2, p. 412.

91 Black, J., and Green,A., Gods, Demons and Symbols of Ancient Mesopotamia – An Illustrated Dictionary. British Museum Press, London, 1992, p.173.

92 Wilhelm, Joseph. "The Nicene Creed." The Catholic Encyclopedia. Vol. 11. New York: Robert Appleton Company, 1911. 25 Nov. 2012<http://www.newadvent.org/cathen/11049a.htm>.

93 The Catholic Encyclopedia. New York: Robert Appleton Company. Retrieved November 25, 2012 from New Advent: http://www.newadvent.org/cathen/12174a.htm

94 McGrath, *A Brief History of Heaven*, 167.

95 Rowan Williams. Tokens of Trust: An Introduction to Christian Belief. (Westminster: John Knox Press, 2007) 155.

96 Williams, *Tokens of Trust*, 154 quoting Augustine of Hippo, *City of God*, XXII.30.

97 Wolfgang Heimpel, in "The Sun at Night and the Doors of Heaven in Babylon," *Journal of Cuneiform Studies,* Vol 38, No.2, Autumn, 1986.

98 Heimpel, *Sun at Night*, 130-131.

99 Morse, *The Difference Heaven Makes.*

100 Carole, R. Fontain, "A modern look at ancient wisdom: The Instruction of Ptahhotep Revised", *The Biblical Archaeologist*, 44, No.3 1981, 157.

101 Andrew A. Gordon, "The Ka as an Animating Force," *Journal of the American Research Center in Egypt*, Vol.33, 1996.

102 Zabkar, *Herodotus and the Egyptian Idea of Immortality,* 61.

103 Smith, *Osiris and the Deceased*, 2.

104 Barr, *Question of Religious Influence*, 229.

105 Pagels, *Gnostic Paul*, 5.

106 Heimpel, 146.

107 Tertullian, *Apologeticus.*

108 J. Sollier, "The Communion of Saints." *The Catholic Encyclopedia* Vol.4. New York: Robert Appleton Company, 1908.

109 McGrath, A *Brief History of Heaven,* 166.

110 Russell, *5.*

References

Arbel, Vita Daphna. *Beholders of Divine Secrets: Mysticism and Myth in the Hekhalot and Merkavah Literature.* New York: State University of New York Press, 2003.

Aristophanes. "Peace." In *The Complete Greek Drama*, 2. edited by Eugene O'Neill, 830-840. New York, NY: Random House, 1938.

Aristotle. *On the Heavens.* Translated by J. L. Stocks, Oxford, The Clarendon press, 1922.

Ashton, John. *The Religion of Paul the Apostle.* New Haven: Yale University Press, 2000.

Barr, James. "The Question of Religious Influence: The Case of Zoroastrianism, Judaism, and Christianity." *Journal of the American Academy of Religion*, 53, No. 2 (1985): 201-235.

Beck, R. "The Mysteries of Mithras: A New Account of Their Genesis." *Journal of Roman Studies*, 88 (1998): 115-128.

Beck, R. "Ritual, Myth, Doctrine and Initiation in the Mysteries of Mithras: New Evidence from a Cult Vessel." *Journal of Roman Studies*, 90, 2000:145-180.

Betz, Hans Dieter. *The Greek Magical Papyri in Translation, including the Demotic Spells, Vol 1.* Chicago: University of Chicago Press, 1992.

Boyce, Mary. *Zoroastrians: Their Religious Beliefs and Practices.* London: Routledge, 1979, 2001.

Boyle, Marjorie O'Rourke. "Pure of Heart: From Ancient Rites to Renaissance Plato." *Journal of the History of Ideas*, 63, no. 1 (2002): 41-62.

Bucur, Bogdan G. "Hierarchy, Prophecy, and the Angelomorphic Spirit: A Contribution to the Study of the Book of Revelation's "Wirkungsgeschichte"." *Journal of Biblical Literature*, 127, no. 1 (2008): 73-194.

Campion, Nicholas. *The Dawn of Astrology: A Cultural History of Western Astrology, 1: The Ancient and Classical Worlds.* London: Continuum Books, 2008.

Campion, Nicholas. *Astrology and Cosmology in the World's Religions.* New York: New York University Press, 2012.

Charles, R.H. (ed.). *The Book of the Secrets of Enoch*, W.R. Morfill (Trans.) Filiquarian Publishing, 2006.

Charlesworth, J. H. (ed.). *The Dead Sea Scrolls, Vol 4B: Angelic Liturgy.* Westminster: John Knox Press, 1999.

Charlesworth, J. H. "Jewish astrology in the Talmud, Pseudepigrapha, the Dead Sea Scrolls, and Early Palestinian Synagogues." *Harvard Theological Review*, Vol.70, No.3/4 (1977):183- 200.

Collins, J.J. *Apocalypse: Morphology of a Genre.* Missoula, MT: Scholars Press,1979.

Cumont, Franz. "Astrology and Religion among the Greeks and Romans." *American lectures on the history of religions. Series of 1911-1912.* New York and London: G. P. Putnam's Sons, 1912.

Dassow, Eva Von (ed.). translated by Raymond Faulkner, foreword by James Wasserman. *The Egyptian Book of the Dead: The Book of Going Forth by Day.* San Francisco: Chronicle Books, 1994 (2008).

Daube, David. "On Acts 23: Sadducees and Angels." *Journal of Biblical Literature*, 109, no. 3, (1990): 493-497.

Davies, Philip R. "Eschatology at Qumran." *Journal of Biblical Literature*, 104, no. 1 (1985): 39- 55.

Davila, James R. *Liturgical Works: Eerdman's Commentaries on the Dead Sea Scrolls.* Michigan: Eerdmans Publishing, 2000.

Eliade, M. *Shamanism: Archaic Techniques of Ecstasy.* Princeton: Bollingen Paperbacks, 1951 (2004).

Eliade, M. *The Sacred and the Profane: The Nature of Religion.* New York, NY: Harcourt, 1957 (1987).

Elior, Rachel. *The Three Temples: On the Emergence of Jewish Mysticism,* translated by David Louvish. Portland: Littman Library of Jewish Civilization, 2005.

Ellington, Dustin W. "The Religion of Paul the Apostle by John Ashton, Review." *Journal of Biblical Literature,* 121, no. 4 (2002): 774-777.

Evelyn-White, Hugh G. (trans). *The Homeric Hymns and Homerica,* Cambridge, MA. London: Harvard University Press, 1914.

Faulker, R.O. *The Ancient Egyptian Coffin Texts.* Vol. 1-II. Stilwell, KS: Digireads, 1973 (2007).

Fletcher-Louis, Crispin. *All the Glory of Adam: Liturgical Anthropology in the Dead Sea Scrolls.* Leiden: E.J. Brill, 2002.

Josephus, Flavius. *The Works of Flavius Josephus,* trans. William Whiston (1737).ö
http://www.sacred-texts.com/jud/josephus/hades.htm

Gieschen, Charles A. *Angelomorphic Christology: Antecedents and Early Evidence.* Leiden: Brill, 1998.

Gershevitch, I. (trans.). *The Avestan Hymn to Mithra.* University of Cambridge Oriental Publications, no.4. Cambridge: University Press, 1959 (1967).

Greig, Alison, 'Angelomorphism and Magical Transformation in the Christian and Jewish Traditions', Celestial Magic, special issue of Culture and Cosmos, Vol. 19, nos. 1 and 2, 2015, pp. 129-44.

Harrison, J.R. "Quest of the Third Heaven: Paul and His Apocalyptic Imitators." *Vigiliae Christianae,* 58, no. 1 (2004): 24-55.

Haug, Martin (trans.). "The Book of Arda Viraf." In *Sacred Books and Early Literature of the East, Volume VII: Ancient Persia,* edited by Charles F. Horne. Bombay: Govt. Central Book Depot, 1872, 1917.

Himmelfarb, Martha. *Ascent to Heaven in Jewish and Christian Apocalypses.* New York: Oxford University Press, 1993.

Homer. *The Odyssey*. Edited by Samuel Butler in Perseus Digital Library, Tufts University.

Horne, Charles. "Ancient Persia". In *The Sacred Books and Early Literature of the East*. New York: Parke, Austin and Lipscomb, 1917.

Irenaeus. "On the Final Restoration of Creation." In The Christian Theology Reader edited by Alister E. McGrath, (Oxford: Blackwell Publishing, 1995 (2001)): 611.

Jastrow, Morris and Albert T. Clay. *An Old Babylonian version of the Gilgamesh Epic*. New Haven: Yale University Press, 1920.

Lewis, I. M. *Religion in Context: Cults and Charisma*. Cambridge: Cambridge University Press, 1996.

Liebeschuetz, Wolf. "The Rise and Fall of the Afterlife. The 1995 Read-Tuckwell Lecture at the University of Bristol by J. N. Bremmer." *Journal of Roman Studies* 94 (2004): 208.

McCurdy, G. H. "Platonic Orphism in the Testament of Abraham." *Journal of Biblical Literature*, no. 61 (1942): 213- 226.

McDannell, Colleen and Bernhard Lang. *Heaven: A History*. New Haven: Yale University Press, 1988 (2001).

McGrath, Alister E. *A Brief History of Heaven*. Malden, MA : Wiley-Blackwell, 2003.

McGrath, Alister E. (ed.). *The Christian Theology Reader*. Oxford: Blackwell Publishing, 1995 (2001).

McKay, J. *Religion in Judah under the Assyrians*. London: SCM Press, 1973.

Mead, G.R.S. (trans.) *Pistis Sophia*. London: J.M.Watkins, 1921.

Morse, Christopher. *The Difference Heaven Makes: Rehearing the Gospel as News*. London: T&T Clark International, 2010.

Mercer, Samuel A.B. *The Pyramid Texts*. New York: Longmans, Green & Co, 1952.

Meyer, M.W. (ed. & trans.). "The Mithras Liturgy." In the *Paris Codex*. http://www.hermetic.com/pgm/mithras-liturgy.html

Mills, L.H. (trans.). "The Zend-Avesta, part III." In *The Yasna, Visparad, Afrinagan, Gahs and Miscellaneous Fragments*, XXXI. Oxford: 1887 (1965).

Mills, L.H. (trans.). "Yasna." In *Sacred Books of the East*. American Edition, 1898.

Morse, Christopher. *The Difference Heaven Makes: Rehearing the Gospel as News*. London:T&T Clark International, 2010.

Mount, Christopher. "1 Corinthians 11:3-16: Spirit Possession and Authority in a Non-Pauline Interpolation."*Journal of Biblical Literature*, 124, no. 2 (2005): 316-328.

Neale, Mary C. *To Heaven and Back. A Doctor's Extraordinary Account of Her Death, Heaven, Angels, and Life Again: A True Story*. Colorado Springs: WaterBrook Press, 2012.

Nickelsburg, George W.E. and James C. VanderKam. *1 Enoch: A New Translation*. Minneapolis: Fortress Press, 2004.

New Revised Standard Version Bible. Division of Christian Education of the National Council of the Churches of Christ in the United States of America. San Francisco, CA: HarperCollins, 1989.

Noel, Daniel C. *The Soul of Shamanism*. New York: Continuum, 1999.

Odeburg, Hugo (ed., trans.). *The Book of Enoch by R. Ishmael Ben Elisha*, http://www.archive.org/details/HebrewBookOfEnochenoch3

Oppenheim, A.L. "A Babylonian Diviners Manual." *Journal of Near Eastern Studies* 33, (1974): 197-220.

Pagels, Elaine. *The Gnostic Paul – Gnostic Exegesis of the Pauline Letters*. New York, NY: Continuum International Publishing Group, 1992.

Plato. "Timaeus." In *Plato in Twelve Volumes*, 9, translated by W.R.M. Lamb. Cambridge, MA: Harvard University Press, 1925.

Plato. *The Republic*. James Adam (trans.). Cambridge: Cambridge University Press, 1902.

Plato. *Gorgias*. Translated by Benjamin Jowet. New York: C. Scribner's Sons, 1871.

Pindar. *Odes*. Translated by Diane Arnson Svarlien. Perseus Digital Library, Tufts University, 1990. http://www.perseus.tufts.edu

Porphyry. *On the Cave of the Nymphs*. Translated by Thomas Taylor. London: Neill and Co. 1917.

Peters, Larry G. "Trance, Initiation, and Psychotherapy in Tamang Shamanism." *American Ethnologist*, 9, No. 1 (1982): 21-46.

Raphael, Simcha Paull. *Jewish Views of the Afterlife*. Plymouth, UK: Rowman & Littlefield Publishers, 2009.

Schaff, Philip and Henry Wace (ed.s). "The Seven Ecumenical Councils." In *Nicene and Post- Nicene Fathers of the Christian Church*, Second Series, XVI. Michigan: WM. B. Eerdmans, 1901, (2010).

Poythress, Vern Sheridan. *Journal of the Evangelical Theological Society* 36 (1993): 41-54.

Reiner, Erica and David Pingree. *Babylonian Planetary Omens 2*. Malibu: Undena Publications, 1981.

Russell, Jeffrey Burton. *A History of Heaven – The Singing Silence*. Princeton: Princeton University Press, 1997.

Scott, Alan. *Origen and the life of the Stars: A History of an Idea*. Clarendon: Oxford University Press, 2001.

Scott, Walter. "The Ancient Greek and Latin Writings Which Contain Religious or Philosophic Teachings Ascribed to Hermes Trismegistus" *Hermetica*, Vol. 1, Libellus I.25, 129. Boston, Massachusetts: Shambhala, 1985.

Segal, Alan F. *Life after death: A history of the Afterlife in the Religions of the West*. New York: Doubleday, 2003.

Shirokogoroff, S. *Psychomental Complex of the Tungus*. London: Routledge & Kegan Paul, 1935.

Smith, Mark. "Osiris and the Deceased," *Encyclopedia of Egyptology,* 2008.

Smith, Mark. "Democratization of the Afterlife," *Encyclopedia of Egyptology,* 2009.

Smith, C. Michael. *Jung and Shamanism in Dialogue: Retrieving the Soul/Retrieving the Sacred*. Victoria B.C., Canada: Trafford Publishing, 2007.

Smith, Morton (trans.). *Hekhalot Rabbati: The Greater Treatise concerning the Palaces of Heaven,* edited by Don Karr, corrected by Gershom Scholem. Morton Smith Estate: Digital Brilliance, 1943-7 (2009).

Smith, Wilfred Cantwell. *Faith and Belief.* Princeton: Princeton University Press, 1979 (1998).

Smith, Wilfred Cantwell. *The meaning and end of religion.* New York: Harper and Row, 1978 (1962).

Stilwell, Gary A. *Afterlife – Postmortem Judgments in Ancient Egypt and Ancient Greece*, Lincoln: iUniverse, 2005.

Scholem, Gershom. *Major Trends in Jewish Mysticism*. New York: Schocken Books, 1946 (1995).

Taylor, John H. (ed.). *Ancient Egyptian Book of the Dead: Journey through the afterlife.* London: British Museum Press, 2010.

Tertullian. *Tertullian: Adversus Marcionem* edited and translated by Ernest Evans. London: Oxford University Press, 1972.

Tertullian. "Prescription Against Heretics" In *Ante-Nicene Fathers*, Vol. 3. Translated by Peter Holmes, edited by Alexander Roberts, James Donaldson, and A. Cleveland Coxe, 24- 30. Buffalo, NY: Christian Literature Publishing Co., 1885. Revised and edited for New Advent by Kevin Knight. <http://www.newadvent.org/fathers/0311.htm>.

Tertullian. "On Hell and Heaven." In *The Christian Theology Reader* edited by Alister E. McGrath, 614. Oxford: Blackwell Publishing, 1995 (2001).

Tertullian. "On the Millennium." In *The Christian Theology Reader* edited by Alister E. McGrath, 615. Oxford: Blackwell Publishing, 1995 (2001).

Tufts University. *Perseus Digital Library.*
http://www.perseus.tufts.edu/hopper/collection?collection=Perseus:collection:Greco-Roman

Tupper, Kenneth, W. "Entheogens and Existential Intelligence: The use of Plant Teachers as Cognitive Tools," *Canadian Journal of Education*, 27, no.4 (2002): 499-515.

Ulansay, David. *The origins of the Mithraic mysteries: Cosmology and salvation in the ancient world*. Oxford: Oxford University Press, 1989.

Wallis, Robert J. *Shamans/Neo-Shamans*. London: Routledge, 2003.

Wente, Edward F. "Mysticism in Pharaonic Egypt." *Journal of Near Eastern Studies*, 41, no. 3 (1982): 161-179.

Wilhelm, Joseph. "The Nicene Creed." In *The Catholic Encyclopedia* Vol. 11. New York: Robert Appleton Company, 1911.

Williams, Rowan. *Tokens of Trust: An Introduction to Christian Belief.* Westminster: John Knox Press, 2007.

Wright, J.E. *The Early History of Heaven*. New York: Oxford University Press, 2000.

Wyatt, N. *The Mythic Mind: Essays on Cosmology and Religion in Ugaritic and Old Testament Literature*. London: Equinox Publishing, 2005.

Zabkar, Louis V. "Herodotus and the Egyptian Idea of Immortality," *Journal of Near Eastern Studies* 22, no.1 (1963): 57-63.

Zaehner, R.C. *The Dawn and Twilight of Zoroastrianism*. Whitefish, MT: Literary Licensing, 2011.

Zweifel, Thomas D. and Aaron L. Raskin. *The Rabbi and the CEO: The Ten Commandments for 21st Century Leaders*. New York: Select Books, 2008.

Printed in the United States
By Bookmasters